D1159535

LEADERS OF RELIGION

General Editor

Reverend Professor C. W. Dugmore, D.D.

John Henry Newman

John Henry Newman

CHARLES STEPHEN DESSAIN
of the Birmingham Oratory

NELSON

THOMAS NELSON AND SONS LTD
36 Park Street London W1
P.O. Box 336 Apapa Lagos
P.O. Box 25012 Nairobi
77 Coffee Street San Fernando Trinidad

Thomas Nelson (Australia) Ltd
597 Little Collins Street Melbourne C2

Thomas Nelson and Sons (South Africa) (Proprietary) Ltd
P.O. Box 9881 Johannesburg

Thomas Nelson and Sons (Canada) Ltd
81 Curlew Drive Don Mills Ontario

Thomas Nelson and Sons
Copewood and Davis Streets Camden 3, N.J.

First published 1966

Printed in Great Britain by
Thomas Nelson (Printers) Ltd, London and Edinburgh

IN REMEMBRANCE OF
FRANCIS JOSEPH BACCHUS

Abbreviations used in the Notes

Apo.	*Apologia pro Vita Sua*
Ari.	*The Arians of the Fourth Century*
A.W.	*John Henry Newman Autobiographical Writings*
Dev.	*An Essay on the Development of Christian Doctrine*
Diff.	*Certain Difficulties felt by Anglicans in Catholic Teaching*
G.A.	*An Essay in Aid of a Grammar of Assent*
Idea	*The Idea of a University*
Jfc.	*Lectures on the Doctrine of Justification*
L. and D.	*The Letters and Diaries of John Henry Newman,* edited by Charles Stephen Dessain
P.S.	*Parochial and Plain Sermons*
S.D.	*Sermons on Subjects of the Day*
U.S.	*Fifteen Sermons preached before the University of Oxford*
V.M.	*The Via Media of the Anglican Church*
Ward	*The Life of John Henry Cardinal Newman*, by Wilfrid Ward

Contents

Introduction

In a sermon preached at Tunbridge Wells on 19 August 1832, at St Mary's Oxford a fortnight later, and published early in 1834 Newman took for his text, 'If ye know these things, happy are ye if ye do them', and immediately commented: 'There never was a people or an age to which these words could be more suitably addressed than to this country at this time; because we know more of the way to serve God, of our duties, our privileges, and our reward, than any other people hitherto, as far as we have the means of judging'.[1] The insularity of this judgment may be partly explained by Newman's still persisting conviction that the Church of Rome was bound up with the cause of Antichrist. Even so, it seems a surprising claim to make for the England of the Industrial Revolution, in the year of the passing of the first Reform Bill. Newman was perhaps abstracting from the atmosphere of crisis, which had existed since the American and French Revolutions. He threw some light on his meaning in another contemporary sermon, when he spoke of the 'fact, that all the rank, and the station, and the intelligence, and the opulence of the country is professedly with religion . . . that the institutions of the country are based on the acknowledgment of religion as true'.[2] As an old man in 1874, in his controversy with Gladstone, he exclaimed, 'When I was young the State had a conscience, and the Chief Justice of the day pronounced, not as a point of obsolete law, but as an energetic living truth, that Christianity was the law of the land'.[3] But Newman meant much more than this. If 'the Bible is the religion of Protestants', who use their private judgment to

1. *Parochial and Plain Sermons*, henceforth abbreviated *P.S.*, I, p. 27. Quotations from Newman's works are always, unless otherwise stated, from his uniform edition, which was begun in 1868 with *Parochial and Plain Sermons*, and concluded in 1881 with *Select Treatises of St Athanasius*. From 1886 until the stock was destroyed in World War II, the volumes were published in London, by Longmans, Green and Co.
2. *P. S.*, I, p. 59
3. *A Letter to the Duke of Norfolk* in *Certain Difficulties felt by Anglicans in Catholic Teaching*, abbreviated as *Diff.*, II, p. 264

interpret it, then we may say that Protestantism in the third decade of the nineteenth century was a greater force in the lives of Englishmen than at any time before or since. During the previous century the Methodist preaching had spread an effective Protestantism among the less educated classes, and it had been followed within the Church of England by the Evangelical revival, which had an even wider influence. Although this was losing impetus by the eighteen-thirties, it was still extending its conquests, especially in the middle and richer classes. It was giving a more refined tone to society in general, and making the English Sunday stricter. When all this was compared with the infidel excesses which spread over Europe from revolutionary France, England seemed a very Christian country. Newman in later life said of Evangelicalism that it 'had been a great blessing for England; it had brought home to the hearts of thousands the cardinal and vital truths of Revelation'.[1] It proclaimed the necessity of personal religion, of devotion to the Saviour of sinners, and of an experience of conversion. It can be compared with the Franciscan revival or the 'New Devotion' in the Low Countries. But it was Protestant in its stress on religious experience, on the subjective reaction of the believer, who was to aim at a 'spiritual-mindedness' he was soon anxious to bring others to share. The dangers of a religion that encouraged the contemplation of self were obvious—it could degenerate into cant and hypocrisy. Among the evidence that this was a result is that of the great novelists. There are Pecksniff, Mr Brocklehurst, Lady Southdown, Mrs Proudie and many others, to represent this side of Evangelicalism. What was even more dangerous for the future, concentration on the feelings of the heart led to a disparagement of the external and objective in religion, creeds, sacraments and the visible Church. A man's feelings were more important than his beliefs. Theology and the intellectual basis of religion were undervalued, so that the way lay open for rationalism. As yet the latitudinarian party lacked influence, and while it laid less stress on dogma than the Evangelicals, they shared the same vague conception of the Church. Soon Thomas Arnold was to propose to include in it all Christians except Romanists, by way of averting disestablishment.

1. *John Henry Newman Autobiographical Writings*, edited by Henry Tristram, London 1956, abbreviated as *A.W.*, p. 79

Although there were dangers ahead, for the moment Evangelicalism was extremely powerful. Under its auspices, societies were founded to remedy every temporal and spiritual ill. Money was poured into them, and the Bible and Missionary Societies spread the Evangelical teaching through the colonies. Against this picture of a widespread and influential Protestantism may be set the popular hatred aroused by the opposition of the bishops to the Reform Bill, and by the pluralism and wealth of the Anglican Church. But for the most part this hatred was not against religion, but against a religious corporation, which was regarded as a privileged department of the State. The right of the civil power to control the Church was taken for granted, and an Erastian view was common to most shades of opinion in the Church of England. In a very practical way Christianity was the law of the land. Very soon, by a typical English compromise, the State was to appoint Ecclesiastical Commissioners, who would ensure on the one hand that pluralism and similar abuses were ended, and on the other that the wealth of the Church was not confiscated, but redistributed within itself.

The only group which really regarded the Church as a divine institution independent of the State, the extreme High Church party, was very small. It still held the doctrine of the apostolic succession, but made little impact on the rest of Anglicans or on society generally. In ritual matters it was Protestant, and did not, for instance, use the vestments sanctioned by the *Book of Common Prayer*. Its members were to be found in a few country parsonages and cathedral cities. In 1834 Newman remarked that W. F. Hook at Coventry was the only High Church vicar in any large town, and he found himself exposed to considerable opposition from the Evangelicals there.

Protestant Christianity held sway among the English people, and was the origin of much piety, morality and philanthropy, the latter, alas, sometimes harsh and patronising. English Protestantism was strongly anti-Catholic, and many seriously held that the Roman Church was bound up with the cause of Antichrist. The Evangelicals could furnish no real intellectual defence of their religion. The latitudinarians, on the other hand, relied on a superficial natural theology. Both parties recited the Creed and professed belief in the Catholic Church, but neither noun nor adjective had any very precise meaning.

The Christian religion claims to be divinely revealed, and only in so far as it holds faithfully to the teaching of its Revealer can it be fully effective. If the message becomes altered or exaggerated, to that extent it is liable to fail, to present a caricature of its true self, and to deter those who should be drawn to it. There was plenty of Christianity in England in 1832, enough to make Newman say 'we know more of the way to serve God than any other people hitherto', but how much that was essential was lacking, and how much there was to put off the sincere seeker!

The fundamental interest of Newman's life is his devotion to the cause of Revealed Religion. He was led to accept it wholeheartedly as a boy, and to seek out its full and balanced content. This devotion gave his life its unity. It led him to become the leader in a movement to reinvigorate and supernaturalise the Church of England; it caused him to abandon it for the Roman Church; it made him try to remedy various deficiencies he found there, and to moderate excesses. In many of his efforts he failed at the time, but history has vindicated him, and the Catholic movement of reform has hailed him as a prophet. He was always a herald of forgotten truths. How did he discover them, and how was he enabled to set out in such catholic fulness the Revealed Religion of Christianity?

CHAPTER I

The First Thirty Years (1801-32)

JOHN HENRY NEWMAN was born at 80 Old Broad Street, in the City of London, on 21 February 1801, and died at the Oratory, Birmingham, on 11 August 1890. His father, a London banker, broadminded in religion, disliked Evangelicalism and religious enthusiasm. His mother, Jemima Fourdrinier, of a Huguenot family driven from France after the revocation of the Edict of Nantes, taught her son that 'Bible Religion', which he would one day in his *Grammar of Assent* call 'both the recognised title and the best description of English religion'. It consisted 'not in rites or creeds, but mainly in having the Bible read in Church, in the family, and in private'. It gave the English people religious thoughts, a high moral standard and a sense of God's Providence over men. It was 'not a religion of persons and things, of acts of faith and of direct devotion; but of sacred scenes and pious sentiments'.[1] Thus although he had been taught his Anglican catechism, Newman could say that he had, as a boy, 'no formed religious convictions'.[2] But he did know his Bible through and through, which was read to him by his mother and grandmother, before he could read it himself. His parents were practising members of the Church of England, and were untouched by Evangelicalism. Their letters after their marriage in 1799 show them going to 'routs' and plays. Their six lively children, three boys and three girls (John Henry was the eldest), were fond of play-going and play-acting. They grew up in solid comfort and their literary, musical and artistic talents were given every encouragement.

In May 1808 John went as a boarder with his brother Charles, to the large private school of two to three hundred boys, founded at Ealing in the seventeenth century, of which Dr George Nicholas

1. *An Essay in aid of a Grammar of Assent*, abbreviated as *G.A.*, pp. 56–7
2. *Apologia pro Vita Sua*, abbreviated as *Apo.*, p. 1

was now the owner and the headmaster. Said to be 'conducted on Eton lines', the school was more civilised than the public schools of the time, and although it did not give the same grounding in the classics (the boys left at sixteen), it was educationally more progressive. It is clear from the way Newman later criticised the standards and tuition at Oxford that the foundations of his scholarship were laid at this school. Nicholas, the headmaster, was accustomed to say that no boy had run through the School, from the bottom to the top, so rapidly as John Newman. George Huxley, the father of the scientist, was among the masters, and when Newman left, wrote to him of his pride in being 'instrumental in having prepared the way towards the necessary acquirements your prospects demand. I must not forget to name the unbroken line of good conduct and attention during the whole of your residence here—these I shall remember and in anticipating your future success I am persuaded I do so on rational grounds'. Among Newman's contemporaries at the school were Richard Westmacott, the sculptor, George Selwyn, later Bishop of New Zealand, and Frederick Thesiger, later Lord Chelmsford, who was to be the leading counsel for the prosecution against Newman, in the Achilli trial. Shortly after Newman left, Charles Francis Adams, son and grandson of Presidents of the United States, was sent there by his father, then American minister in London. The school, at which dancing was taught, music encouraged (Newman learned to play the violin), and a play of Terence or Plautus acted in Latin each year, was unaffected by Evangelicalism. Some years after Newman had left, his youngest brother Francis adopted Evangelical views and practices at the school, and underwent various persecutions from his schoolfellows as a result.

Besides distinguishing himself in his studies, Newman emerged as a leader among the boys, editing a magazine and presiding over a club. Success had its temptations.

When I was fourteen I read Paine's *Tracts against the Old Testament*, and found pleasure in thinking of the objections that were contained in them. Also I read some of Hume's *Essays*; and perhaps that on *Miracles*. So at least I gave my father to understand; but perhaps it was a brag. Also I recollect copying out some French verses, perhaps Voltaire's, against the immortality of the soul, and saying to myself something like 'How dreadful but how plausible.'[1]

1. *Apo.*, p. 3

That was a public statement in the *Apologia*. Already in a private notebook in 1823 he wrote, 'I recollect (in 1815 I believe) thinking I should like to be virtuous, but not religious. There was something in the latter idea I did not like. Nor did I see the *meaning* of loving God'.[1] Newman's was not yet 'a religion of persons'. Now, however, came the turning-point of his life, mentioned in a score of places in his writings, both published and unpublished—his first conversion. In the *Apologia* he wrote:

> When I was fifteen (in the autumn of 1816,) a great change of thought took place in me. I fell under the influence of a definite Creed, and received into my intellect impressions of dogma, which through God's mercy, have never been effaced or obscured.[2]

Adversity prepared the way for this 'great change of thought'. On 8 March 1816 the bank of which Newman's father was a partner, was obliged to suspend payment, in the financial crisis after the Napoleonic Wars. Creditors were paid in full within a month, but the bank was closed, and Mr Newman's prosperity was at an end. His London house was let, his country cottage at Norwood sold, and he began to earn a precarious living as the manager of a brewery at Alton in Hampshire. Meanwhile, during the summer, his son was struck down by a serious illness, of which he wrote long after in his journal that 'it made me a Christian—with experiences before and after, awful and known only to God'.[3] Dr Nicholas proved a friend in need, and Newman was allowed to remain at school during the summer holidays, to convalesce, and to be out of the way while his family made their new dispositions. There also remained at the school during the holidays, a young classics master, Walter Mayers, a clergyman of twenty-six, who had recently undergone conversion and become an Evangelical. In the *Apologia* Newman called him 'the human means of the beginning of divine faith in me'. With his school friends away, there was time for reflection and for Mayers' words and influence to make themselves felt. Newman noted the exact dates of the great change of thought: 'the first or last days of the half year of my conversion, August 1 and December 21, 1816.'[4] Great as was Newman's debt to Mayers, he tells us he was even more influenced by the books he placed in his hands, and above

1. *A.W.*, p. 169
2. *Apo.*, p. 4
3. *A.W.*, p. 268
4. *A.W.*, p. 181

all, 'by the writer who made a deeper impression on my mind than any other, and to whom (humanly speaking) I almost owe my soul—Thomas Scott'. From being a Deist, Scott, after a long search and struggle with himself, was eventually drawn to Christianity in its milder Calvinistic form. He described his theological development and beliefs in *The Force of Truth*, 1779. He was Rector of Aston Sandford in Buckinghamshire from 1801, until his dedicated life ended in 1821. In the *Apologia* Newman praised Scott's 'bold unworldliness and vigorous independence of mind. He followed truth wherever it lead him, beginning with Unitarianism and ending with a zealous faith in the Holy Trinity. It was he who first planted deep in my mind that fundamental truth of religion'. The teaching on the Blessed Trinity, the Incarnation, and the Redemption became a reality, as is shown by the prayers Newman now composed for his private use; and he tried to live up to the doctrine of the presence and indwelling of the Holy Spirit in the soul, on which Scott insisted. He gave full assent to the belief in eternal happiness, as well as in 'eternal punishment as delivered by our Lord Himself'. From the Calvinist books he read Newman learned the 'Catholic doctrine of the warfare between the city of God and the powers of darkness'. He also accepted from the same source that after his conversion he was predestined to eternal glory. But this idea did not have the effect of making him careless, and by the time he was twenty-one it had faded away. What he called the 'detestable doctrine' of predestination to eternal death, Newman never made his own, and it was also one that Scott simply rejected.[1]

Newman now became an Evangelical, but his seems not to have been a conventional Evangelical conversion. It was long drawn out, not sudden, and it was not accompanied by the special emotional experiences that Evangelical teaching considered so important. His feelings were not violent and he was forced to admit that they differed from the descriptions of conversion that he now read in books. Evangelicals were to doubt whether he had really been converted at all. Newman called his experience 'a change of thought' to emphasise its intellectual character, and he already glimpsed what was to be the rational justification of his new certitudes. He was struck by their reflex character, 'I know that I know', and by their consistency, the hall-mark of truth—

1. *Apo.*, pp. 4–6

a *Grammar of Assent* in embryo.[1] He also drew up painstaking lists of Scripture texts in support of the doctrine of the Holy Trinity, and others for each verse of the Athanasian Creed. He would study to the full the Revealed Religion which he had now made his own. With intellectual conviction went the wholehearted acceptance of the Gospel ideal of holiness. He began to live more strictly and to try to attend to God's presence, to 'rest in the thought of two and two only absolute and luminously self-evident beings, myself and my Creator'. The visible world, so beautiful and significant, seemed less real than that which was unseen. This was not a kind of incipient idealism, but a deep *Christian* way of thinking. His objective Trinitarian faith kept him from the subjective contemplation of himself, and indeed he was naturally a man of action. He made two of Scott's sayings his own, 'Holiness rather than peace', and 'Growth the only evidence of life'. Just before his conversion period was over, he went with his father to Oxford and was entered at Trinity College. He did not go into residence properly until the following October. The intervening months, those immediately after his conversion, were spent in hard study. He had now to make his way in the world, and his talents were to be used in God's service.

Another change came over him, which was not a usual concomitant of an Evangelical conversion, the 'deep imagination' which took possession of him in the autumn of 1816 that it would be God's will that he should lead a single life. This was more or less connected with the idea that his life's work would require such a sacrifice. For a parallel with Newman's first conversion, one might imagine a gifted unthinking boy for whom a retreat at school or the reading of some religious classic marked the beginning of a spiritual life, except that Newman speaks much more strongly. He was 'made a Christian', he began a new life. He accepted Revealed Religion in the purest form available to him, and gave himself to God in consequence. It was the turning-point which was to give the rest of his life its unity. His unfolding mind was captured by the Christian Revelation, and his heart by the Christian ideal of holiness.

In October 1817, at the age of sixteen and a half, Newman came into residence at Oxford, which he was to describe a quarter

1. *A.W.*, p. 150

of a century later as 'the most religious university in the world'.[1] Every undergraduate had to subscribe to the Thirty-nine Articles, so that only Anglicans could be admitted to it. Most of the Fellows of the Colleges were required to take Orders if they wished to retain their Fellowships, and they had to relinquish them on marriage. Although there was no Faculty of Theology at either Oxford or Cambridge, these two Universities between them provided the vast majority of the clergymen of the Established Church. A very much larger proportion of graduates entered the Anglican ministry than any other profession. This is not to say that Oxford in any other way resembled a seminary. The morals and customs of the eighteenth century were not extinct, and at Trinity College Newman's Evangelical resolutions were put to the test. He lived a life of prayer, recollection and hard work, but Trinity had little influence on his religious development. In November 1817 he made his first communion, in the College chapel, which he always admired and of which he had a picture in his room to the end of his days. The College was to him 'a very dear place, but a very idle one',[2] and as was to be the case with him throughout his life, he made many friends there. The chief of these was John William Bowden, of a wealthy family in the Isle of Wight, who later became a Commissioner of Stamps and Taxes, and as a devout Anglican layman wrote a life of Gregory VII. Together at Trinity they edited anonymously a periodical, *The Undergraduate,* and composed a romantic poem, *St Bartholomew's Eve*, about a Protestant gentleman and a Catholic lady, which ended in the death of both, through the machinations of a fanatical priest.

In 1818 Newman won a College scholarship of £60 a year, tenable for nine years, and this was important for him, in view of the parlous state of his family's finances. His final examinations were in 1820. and he was expected to get a 'double first', but, owing to overwork and excitement, he broke down and had to retire, having succeeded only in making sure of his B.A. degree. This was not merely a personal disappointment, but a great blow, because it made it more unlikely that he would be able soon to support his family. In spite of misgivings about his ambition, he decided to retrieve the situation by sitting for a Fellowship at

1. *Essays Critical and Historical*, II, p. 409
2. *Historical Sketches*, III, p. 316

Oriel College, then outstanding, and at the height of its literary and intellectual fame. He was elected to a Fellowship on 12 April 1822, and the company into which he was now introduced had a decisive influence on his development. Newman called it 'of all days most memorable. It raised me from obscurity and need to competency and reputation'.[1] He now had an assured income, but he also nearly worked himself to death with private pupils in order to be able to send money to his family. At the end of 1821 his father had been declared a bankrupt and the house in Southampton Street was sold. Three years later he died. Meanwhile in 1822, his youngest son, Francis, came up to Worcester College, and John paid all his expenses, besides contributing largely to the support of his mother and three sisters.

Now, in the liberal atmosphere of the Oriel Common-room, Newman 'came out of his shell'. He was put into the hands of Richard Whately, later Archbishop of Dublin, who had recently relinquished an Oriel Fellowship, on marriage. Newman described him as 'free and easy in manners, rough indeed and dogmatic in his enunciation of opinion, but singularly gracious to undergraduates and young masters, who, if they were worth anything, were only too happy to be knocked about in argument by such a man'.[2] Whately in his turn described Newman as the most clear-headed man he knew, and made use of him in composing his *Elements of Logic*. Whately was a latitudinarian, but also anti-Erastian, and from him Newman learned 'the idea of the Christian Church, as a divine appointment, and as a substantive visible body, independent of the State, and endowed with rights, prerogatives, and powers of its own'.[3]

Already in January 1822, before he won his Oriel Fellowship, Newman had made up his mind to seek Anglican Orders. He was made Deacon on 13 June 1824, and on that day wrote in his journal:

> It is over. I am thine O Lord. . . . At first, after the hands were laid on me, my heart shuddered within me; the words 'for ever' are so terrible. It was hardly a good feeling that made me feel melancholy at the idea of giving up all for God. At times indeed my heart burned within me, particularly during the singing of the *Veni Creator*. Yet Lord, I ask not for comfort in comparison with sanctification.

1. *A.W.*, p. 63
2. *A.W.*, p. 66
3. *A.W.*, p. 69

The following day he added a sentence which gives the real key to his actions henceforward, 'I have the responsibility of souls on me to the day of my death'.[1] All his undertakings would have a pastoral purpose.

He long had thoughts of becoming a missionary and made renewed inquiries on the subject with the Church Missionary Society shortly after his ordination. In the meantime he accepted the curacy of the poor parish of St Clement, beyond Magdalen Bridge, at Oxford, as his title for ordination, and he began work there in July 1824.

It was now that Newman's Evangelical doctrines melted away. Edward Hawkins, one of the Oriel Fellows, was Vicar of St Mary's, the University Church. Newman showed him his proposed first sermon, and Hawkins criticised it severely because it divided men into two clearly distinct classes, those who had been 'converted' and those who had not. Then Newman himself, besides preaching two sermons on Sundays at St Clement's, began to visit his poor flock, house by house. He had learned to be a realist and always to go by facts, hence he soon discovered that the Evangelical theory did not work. Rather than the Evangelical view that the Church consisted of those who had undergone experience of conversion, Hawkins taught him to accept the doctrine of baptismal regeneration. Baptism was not an empty symbol, but brought within the Church all who received it, even though they were too young to have any experience of what was happening to them. A subjective criterion was rejected in favour of one that was objective. From Hawkins too, Newman learned that the Bible needed to be interpreted and explained by tradition. 'The sacred text was never intended to teach doctrine, but only to prove it.' 'If we would learn doctrine, we must have recourse to the formularies of the Church.'[2] In 1825 Newman read Bishop Butler's *Analogy of Religion*, and was greatly influenced by Butler's insistence on the analogies and similarities between the works of God as seen in nature and as known by revelation. He also taught Newman the doctrine of a visible church, 'the oracle of truth and pattern of sanctity, the duties of external religion, and the historical character of revelation'.[3] Already in these early years at St Clement's Newman was preaching about the 'visibility' of the Church, and about its being 'Catholic' and 'Apostolic'. Samuel Wilberforce, an

1. *A.W.*, pp. 200–1 2. *Apo.*, p. 9 3. *Apo.*, p. 10

Evangelical like his father, the philanthropist, went to hear Newman preach at St Clement's and came away astonished.

At Easter 1826, on being appointed one of the tutors at Oriel, Newman resigned his curacy. At about the same time Richard Hurrell Froude, an ardent High Churchman, was elected a Fellow of the College. Newman being still more or less an Evangelical, although with some of the liberal tendencies of the Oriel Common-room, it was a year at least before the two became close friends. Newman had already come to know and admire another High Churchman, E. B. Pusey, who was elected a Fellow of Oriel in 1823, but he soon left Oxford to pursue his studies in Germany and even dabble there in liberalism. Froude was the disciple of John Keble, and between them they represented the old High Church tradition at its noblest, but Keble, too, had retired from Oriel in 1823, to assist his father in his country rectory at Fairford. Thus it was above all through Hurrell Froude that Newman came into contact with High Church beliefs, although it was Froude's boast that his best deed in life had been to make Newman and Keble understand each other. Froude was one of the first religious Englishmen in the century to have a real understanding and appreciation of the Roman Church. He could not believe that Newman really considered it to be under the influence of Antichrist. He regarded the Church's tradition rather than the Bible as the instrument of religious teaching. He disliked the Reformers and his ideal was the theocratic Church of the Middle Ages. He gradually made Newman see the Reformation in a new light, and look with sympathy towards the Church of Rome. Froude had a high idea of the sanctity demanded of a Christian. It was he who taught Newman to believe in the doctrine of the Real Presence, and to have devotion to the Blessed Virgin. Thanks to Froude, also, Newman accepted the doctrine of the apostolic succession, that the Church and the Bishops derive authority and power from their historic link with the Church of Apostolic times. The old religious High Church teaching, derived from the Anglican divines of the seventeenth century, thus reached Newman through Froude and Keble. But they were the representatives of a very small party in the Church of England.

The natural antagonists and alternative among Anglicans to the Evangelicals, in both the intellectual and the ecclesiastical sphere, were the Liberals (in matters religious), well represented at Oriel by Whately, Thomas Arnold and R. D. Hampden. The old Erastian High and Dry Churchmen were also antagonistic to the Evangelicals, but to them Newman was never attracted. The broadminded Liberals played down the supernatural in religion. Natural goodness and respectability sufficed; little room was left for the intervention of God, and His grace and sacraments were disparaged in consequence. This was the kind of 'liberalism' to which Newman was drawn as his Evangelicalism evaporated. He considered that he was saved from it by his devotion to the ancient Fathers of the Church.

Already at the time of his conversion in 1816, Mr Mayers had given him a copy of the Anglican Joseph Milner's *Church History*, and he had been delighted with the long extracts from St Augustine, St Ambrose, and other Fathers that he found in it. Thus, even as a boy his thoughts had been turned towards the early Church, and he could say (in the last lecture on *Difficulties of Anglicans* in 1850):

> I have never lost, I have never suffered a suspension of the impression deep and most pleasurable which his sketches of St Ambrose and St Augustine left on my mind. From that time the vision of the Fathers was always to my imagination, I may say, a paradise of delight, to the contemplation of which I directed my thoughts.[1]

In the *Apologia* Newman could not remember when he first 'learnt to consider that Antiquity was the true exponent of the doctrines of Christianity and the basis of the Church of England'.[2] At all events, although his liberal tendency somewhat diminished his respect for the Fathers, he made various studies in them from the time he became a Fellow of Oriel, and the first centuries were his *beau ideal* of Christianity. In 1825 he wrote for the *Encyclopaedia Metropolitana* an article on Apollonius of Tyana, and an essay to show the antecedent probability of the miracles in the New Testament. He also planned to write for the *Encyclopaedia* a history of the first three centuries of Christianity. In 1827 he commissioned Pusey in Germany to buy for him as many volumes of the Fathers as he could, and during the long vacation of 1828 he began to read them chronologically, beginning with St Ignatius and St Justin. He read them at first on 'Protestant principles', looking for the controverted doctrines of his own day, and later

1. *Diff.*, I, pp. 370–1 2. *Apo.*, p. 26

felt that he had thus missed half their meaning. Nonetheless, the wholehearted patristic study thus begun enabled Newman gradually to complete his recovery of the full Christian Revelation. He had already studied Holy Scripture, and knew much of it by heart: now the other great treasure-house was laid open to him.

However, even before his new studies could have their full effect upon him, Newman considered that he had been saved from proceeding any distance in the direction of religious liberalism by two events in which he saw God's providential guidance. The first was a severe illness brought on by overwork, in the autumn of 1827, after which he went to convalesce at the house of William Wilberforce. The second was the sudden death of his beloved youngest sister, Mary, at Brighton, where his mother was now living. Newman was devoted to his sisters, but Mary was his favourite, and her death at the age of nineteen, on 5 January 1828, was a grievous blow. It revived in him the vivid sense of the unseen world, invisible but more real than the material universe which acted as its veil. Thinking of Mary he wrote to his sister Jemima: 'What a veil and curtain this world of sense is! beautiful, but still a veil.'[1]

At the end of this fateful month of January Hawkins was elected Provost of Oriel, and Newman took his place as Vicar of the University Church of St Mary. This did not give him any direct responsibility for the University itself. He had a few parishioners in Oxford, but his parish included the poor village of Littlemore, three miles distant, and as yet without a church of its own. Newman soon began to visit his flock there and to catechise the children. In time, his mother and sisters came to live near Littlemore, and in 1835 his mother laid the first stone of a church in the village. However, Newman was far from considering this his only pastoral work. He held his office as tutor of Oriel to be a pastoral one, and this led to a serious difference of opinion with the new Provost. From the time of his appointment as tutor, which was a permanent one, Newman had considered it his duty to use his influence for the spiritual good of those in his charge, and to withstand the rich and aristocratic Gentlemen Commoners, whose behaviour was often scandalous. He was not to be a missionary, but he still had an office in which he must

1. *Letters and Correspondence of John Henry Newman during his Life in the English Church*, edited by Anne Mozley, London 1891, I, p. 184

preach the Gospel. This made him all the more insistent that his pupils should work hard, and be encouraged to do so. Having this object in view, he rearranged the system of study with the other tutors, Robert Wilberforce and Hurrell Froude, and there was a marked rise in the number of Oriel successes in the Schools. But Hawkins, who regarded the tutor's office as a secular one, objected, and refused to assign pupils to the reformers. By 1831 Newman had no more pupils left on his hands, and the number of Oriel first-classes began to fall. Just as this was happening, in April 1831, the publisher, Rivington, asked him to write a book on the early Councils of the Church, to be part of a Theological Library. His pupils, grateful for his devotion, presented him with more volumes of the Fathers, and he set to work, from the primary sources. He soon found he would have to confine himself to the First Council, that of Nicea. As he proceeded he became more and more convinced that the Early Church was the true exponent of the revealed teaching of Christianity. By the end of July 1832 the book was finished. It was published a year later as *The Arians of the Fourth Century*.

This, Newman's first book, deals with far more subjects than its title suggests. Döllinger wrote long afterwards: 'Your work on the Arians will be read and studied in future generations as a model of its kind.'[1] Newman was concerned with one of the great problems of Revealed Religion, the necessity to define and elaborate, as time goes on, the truths given in Holy Scripture. The Council of Nicea provided one of the earliest and most famous examples of the process. Newman admitted that ideally and in the abstract it was better to hold the truths of faith without creeds, formularies and definitions, but from the era of the apostles it had been necessary to draw up the revealed teachings more systematically than they were recorded in Scripture, both for the sake of converts and in order to withstand the attacks of heretics:

The idea of disbelieving, or criticising the great doctrines of the faith, from the nature of the case, would scarcely occur to the primitive Christians. These doctrines were the subject of an Apostolical Tradition; they were the very truths which had been lately revealed to mankind. They had been committed to the Church's keeping, and were dis-

1. Wilfrid Ward, *The Life of John Henry Cardinal Newman* London 1912, abbreviated as *Ward*, I, p. 444

pensed by her to those who sought them, as a favour. They were facts, not opinions.[1]

Thus Newman wrote at the beginning of the second chapter. But once the truths revealed in Scripture were disputed, it was necessary to state them more formally, even at the risk of appearing to explain that to which the human mind is not equal. Early in the third chapter, Newman showed how this came about, when referring to the Emperor Constantine who summoned the Council of Nicea.

Peace is so eminently the perfection of the Christian temper, conduct and discipline . . . that it was almost unavoidable in a heathen soldier and statesman, to regard it as the sole precept of the Gospel. It required a far more refined moral perception, to detect and approve the principle, on which this peace is grounded in Scripture; to submit to the dictation of truth, as such, as a primary authority in matters of political and private conduct; to understand how belief in a certain creed was a condition of divine favour, how the social union was intended to result from a unity of opinions, the love of man to spring from the love of God, and zeal to be prior in the succession of Christian graces to benevolence.

So religious dissensions 'are but the history of truth in its first stage of trial, when it aims at being "pure" before it is "peaceable" '.[2]

Newman laid the blame for the Arian heresy on the School of Antioch, and showed his predilection for the School of Alexandria, Clement, Origen and Athanasius. The account of the teaching of the ante-Nicene Church contains one of the finest expositions in English of the doctrine of the Holy Trinity.[3] Newman made it clear to many of his contemporaries what it meant to believe in a Revealed Religion. This was something to be submitted to and practised, not something to be judged by its effect on the feelings.

In his book Newman sometimes showed a certain youthful intolerance, as he also did in early sermons. He had been one of the minority at Oxford in favour of allowing Catholic emancipation, but when Sir Robert Peel, from being its opponent, turned

1. *The Arians of the Fourth Century*, abbreviated as *Ari.*, p. 134
2. *Ari.*, pp. 243–4
3. *Ari.*, pp. 151–78

right round in support of it, Newman voted against his re-election as member for Oxford in 1829. He did this, however, on academic grounds, because the known views of the University were being overruled. He was influenced also by Froude and Keble, and the incident led to his formal break with the liberal Whately.

CHAPTER 2

The Recovered Christian Truth

By the end of 1832 Newman had recovered in substantial completeness the whole circle of the truths of Revealed Religion. He had now been a Fellow of Oriel for ten years, and his influence, although limited to Oxford and to those connected with it, was considerable. The best men of his college, whether Fellows or not, and some from his first college, gathered round him 'with a curious mixture of freedom, devotion and awe', says R. W. Church, Dean of St Paul's, in his history of the Oxford Movement, 'for with unlimited power of sympathy, he was exacting and even austere in his friendships'. Church, who went to Oxford in 1833, and became Newman's friend, continues: 'These, members of his intimate circle were bound to him not merely by enthusiastic admiration and confidence, but by a tenderness of affection, a mixture of gratitude and reliance of discipleship with the warm love of friendship, of which one has to go back far for examples.'[1] Newman's influence made itself felt by his sermons in St Mary's, which had been going on since 1828. Although he was Vicar of the University Church, he was not preacher to the University. He preached 'parochial sermons' in his small parish. His parishioners for the most part neglected them, but they soon began to be appreciated, especially by the younger graduates and more serious men. There was hardly a studious undergraduate, we are told, who was not affected. Thus, at a time when England really was divided into two nations, Newman began to influence an important section of the educated and ruling class. Most of the descriptions of the sermons in St Mary's and their effect date from the late thirties. To discover their secret at this earlier period we must turn to the sermons themselves. Of the six hundred or so sermons which Newman wrote out as an Anglican, well over half were written before the end of 1832, and when he began to publish

1. R. W. Church, *The Oxford Movement*, London 1892, pp. 131–2

a selection of them, one volume in March 1834, a second in March 1835, and a third completed by the end of the same year, well over half of those printed had been first preached before the end of 1832. The earlier ones he corrected before publication, and they represent his teaching after he had broken with Evangelicalism.[1]

Part of Newman's ascendancy was due to his strictness and holiness of life, which gave authority to his words, part to his earnest practical appeal, and part to his balanced exposition of the Christian dogmas which had gained such a hold on his mind, beginning with his first conversion in 1816. To quote Dean Church once more:

> As tutor at Oriel, Mr Newman had made what efforts he could, sometimes disturbing the authorities, to raise the standard of conduct and feeling among his pupils. When he became a parish priest, his preaching took a singularly practical and plain-spoken character. The first sermon of the series, a typical sermon, 'Holiness necessary for future Blessedness', a sermon which has made many readers grave when they laid it down, was written in 1826, before he came to St Mary's; and as he began so he continued. . . . A passionate and sustained earnestness after a high moral rule, seriously realised in conduct, is the dominant character of these sermons. They showed the strong reaction . . . against the poverty, softness, restlessness, worldliness, the blunted and impaired sense of truth, which reigned with little check in the recognised fashions of professing Christianity; the want of depth both of thought and feeling; the strange blindness to the real sternness, nay the austerity of the New Testament.[2]

Dean Church also remarks, 'The most practical of sermons, the most real in their way of dealing with life and conduct, they are also intensely dogmatic'.[3] It is important to discover what the forgotten dogmas were that Newman thought so momentous, and so in need of being set before his hearers in strongly Protestant England. The most satisfactory way of showing this is to quote from the first three volumes of *Parochial Sermons* and from *The Arians of the Fourth Century*, which were written for the most part before the end of 1832, and all before the end of 1835. Quotations

1. Of Newman's unpublished sermons the great majority are early ones. They are valuable rather for tracing his religious development than for discovering the secret of his influence as the third decade of the century opened.
2. R. W. Church, *The Oxford Movement*, pp. 21–2
3. R. W. Church *Occasional Papers*, II, p. 457

are from the first editions of these works, so that we may see as far as possible what Newman was actually saying at the time. (The references will continue to be to the pages of the uniform edition.) In Newman's own first-edition copies of his sermons, he has inserted various references to the Fathers, which, with the constant quotations from Scripture, bring home how authentic his sources were. In the sermons of this early period we see him with a grasp of the Christian Revelation which was to develop, but not to undergo any fundamental change.

Perhaps the first thing to notice is the breadth of Newman's canvass.

We know well enough for practical purposes what is meant by revealed religion; viz. that it is the doctrine taught in the Mosaic and Christian dispensations, and contained in the holy Scriptures, and is from God in a sense in which no other doctrine can be said to be from Him. Yet, if we would speak correctly, we must confess, on the authority of the Bible itself, that *all* knowledge of religion is from Him, and not only that which the Bible has transmitted to us. There never was a time when God had not spoken to man, and told him to a certain extent his duty. . . . Accordingly we are expressly told in the New Testament, that at no time He left Himself without witness in the world, and that in every nation He accepts those who fear and obey Him. It would seem then, that there is something true and divinely revealed, in every religion all over the earth . . . the distinction . . . is, not that we can and they cannot attain to future blessedness, but that the Church of God ever has had, and the rest of mankind never have had, *authoritative documents* of truth, and *appointed channels* of communication with Him. The Word and the Sacraments are the characteristic of the elect people of God, but all men have had more or less the guidance of tradition, in addition to those internal notices of right and wrong which the Spirit has put into the heart of each individual.[1]

Unfortunately the revealed truths tended to be neglected in the dominant religious party at the time, that of the Evangelicals, and this to most English people was the party to which they must obviously turn if they sought for the Christian religion.

Instead of looking off to Jesus, and thinking little of ourselves, it is at present thought necessary among the mixed multitude of religionists, to examine the heart, with a view of ascertaining whether it is in a spiritual state or no . . . this modern system certainly does disparage the revealed

1. *Ari.*, p. 79–80

doctrines of the Gospel, however its more moderate advocates may shrink from admitting it. Considering a certain state of heart to be the main thing to be aimed at, they avowedly make the Truth as it is in Jesus, the definite Creed of the Church, second in their teaching and profession.

This system 'tends legitimately to obliterate the great Objects brought to light in the Gospel', and 'to throw us back into the vagueness of Heathenism, when many only felt after the Divine Presence; and thus to frustrate the design of Christ's incarnation so far as it is a manifestation of the Unseen Creator'.[1]

At the other extreme, although having a certain similarity in its results, is the religion of a civilised age.

What is the world's religion now? It has taken the brighter side of the Gospel,—its tidings of comfort, its precepts of love; all darker, deeper views of man's condition and prospects being comparatively forgotten. . . . Thus elegance is gradually made the test and standard of virtue, which is no longer thought to possess intrinsic claims on our hearts, or to exist *further than* it leads to the quiet and comfort of others.

Newman continues:

Now I would have you put Christianity out of your thoughts; and consider whether such a state of refinement as I have attempted to describe, is not that to which men might be brought quite independent of religion, by the mere influence of education and civilization.

The danger that threatened was not that of an other-worldly Christianity. Newman went on to admit that many were only partially infected by a worldly spirit, and at bottom, good but imperfect Christians. Still, they dropped the austere side of the Gospel, 'considering it enough to be benevolent, courteous, candid', but with no true zeal for God nor deep hatred of sin, 'no loyalty to the Holy Apostolic Church of which the creed speaks, no sense of the authority of religion as external to the mind; in a word, no seriousness'.[2] As to the Evangelicals: 'They who make self instead of their Maker the great object of their contemplation, will naturally exalt themselves.' They will have rigid predestinarian views, and 'the Scripture doctrines relative to the Church and its offices will be unpalatable to such religionists; nothing being so irreconcilable as the system which makes man's thoughts centre on himself, and that which directs them to a fountain of grace and

1. *P.S.*, II, pp. 163, 166, 168 2. *P.S.*, I, pp. 311–14

truth, on which God has made him dependent'. These principles are 'doubtless antichristian; for they destroy all positive doctrine, all ordinances, all good works, they foster pride, invite hypocrisy, discourage the weak'.[1]

Very different are the foundations of a truly religious life:

To understand that we have souls, is to feel our separation from things visible, our independence of them, our distinct existence in ourselves, our individuality, our power of acting for ourselves this way or that way, our accountableness for what we do. These are the great truths which lie wrapped up indeed even in a child's mind, and which God's grace can unfold there in spite of the influence of the external world; but at first this outward world prevails. We look off from self to the things around us, and forget ourselves in them. Such is our state,—a dependence for support on the reeds which are no stay, and overlooking our real strength,—at a time when God begins His process of reclaiming us to a truer view of our place in His great system of providence. And when He visits us, then in a little while there is a stirring within us. The unprofitableness and feebleness of the things of this world forces itself upon our minds; they promise but cannot perform, they disappoint us. . . . And should it so happen that misfortunes come upon us, (as they often do,) then still more are we led to understand the nothingness of this world; then still more are we led to distrust it, and are weaned from the love of it, till at length it floats before our eyes merely as some idle veil, which, nothwithstanding its many tints, cannot hide the view of what is beyond it; and we begin by degrees to perceive that there are but two beings in the whole universe, our own soul, and the God who made it.

This sermon concluded:

I want a man on the one hand to confess his immortality with his lips, and on the other, to live as if he tried to understand his own words, and then he is in the way of salvation.[2]

Newman was not afraid to speak of sin and its punishment, of the utter purity of God, and of His Judgment. He was full of the realisation that his soul was naked before God, and urged on other souls with the conviction of one who knew.

Newman had learned to appreciate God's presence from the teaching of Walter Mayers and Thomas Scott, and he now began to make this real for others. He understood that the foundation laid in the New Testament for the new life of union with God,

1. *P.S.*, II, pp. 172–3   2. *P.S.*, I, pp. 19–20, 24

which the Christian religion offered to mankind, was the doctrine of the indwelling in the soul of the Holy Spirit, and through Him of the Father and the Son. True Christianity is the presence of Persons. 'God, the Son has graciously vouchsafed to reveal the Father to His creatures from without; God, the Holy Ghost, by inward communications.' He is 'the seal and earnest of an Unseen Saviour; being the present pledge of Him who is absent'. And Newman tries to describe and enable us to realise this Gift. The Holy Ghost 'dwells in body and soul, as in a Temple. Evil spirits indeed have power to possess sinners, but His indwelling is far more perfect; for He is all-knowing and omnipresent, He is able to search into all our thoughts, and penetrate into every motive of the heart. Therefore, He pervades us (if it may be so said) as light pervades a building, or as a sweet perfume the folds of some honourable robe; so that in Scripture language, we are said to be in Him and He in us. It is plain that such an inhabitation brings the Christian into a state altogether new and marvellous, far above the possession of mere gifts'.[1] At the new birth of Baptism the Christian enters the Kingdom of Christ.

By this new birth the Divine Shechinah is set up within him, pervading soul and body separating him really, not only in name, from those who are not Christians, raising him in the scale of being, drawing and fostering into life whatever remains in him of a higher nature.[2]

Newman reminded his hearers that they were temples of God.

We are assured of some real though mystical fellowship with the Father, Son, and Holy Spirit, in order to this; so that both by a real presence in the soul, and by the fruits of grace, God is one with every believer, as in a consecrated Temple. . . .[3]
. . . He who obeys God conscientiously, and lives holily, forces all about him to believe and tremble before the unseen power of Christ. . . . When St Peter's disciple Ignatius, was brought before the Roman Emperor, he called himself Theophorus; and when the emperor asked the feeble old man why he so called himself, Ignatius said, it was because he carried Christ in his breast. . . .[4]

Finally there is the practical conclusion:

. . . For ourselves, in proportion as we realise that higher view of the subject, which we may humbly trust is the true one, let us be careful

1. *P.S.*, II, pp. 217, 220, 222
2. *P.S.*, III, p. 266
3. *P.S.*, II, p. 35
4. *P.S.*, I, pp. 292–3

to act up to it. Let us adore the Sacred Presence within us with all fear, and 'rejoice with trembling'. Let us offer our best gifts in sacrifice to Him who instead of abhorring, has taken up His abode in these sinful hearts of ours. . . . In this then consists our whole duty, to contemplate Almighty God as in heaven, so in our hearts and souls; and again to act the while towards Him and for Him in the works of every day.[1]

Newman showed that he was a preacher of forgotten truths and that he realised the harm of an unbalanced or truncated presentation of Christianity.

It were well if the views I have been setting before you, which in the main are, I trust, those of the Church Catholic from the beginning, were more understood and received among us. They would, please God, put a stop to much of the enthusiasm which prevails on all sides, while they might tend to dispel those cold and ordinary notions of religion which are the opposite extreme. Till we understand that the gifts of grace are unseen, supernatural and mysterious, we have but a choice between explaining away the high and glowing expressions of Scripture, or giving them that rash, irreverent and self-exalting interpretation, which is one of the chief errors of this time. Men of awakened and sensitive minds, knowing from Scripture that the gift of the Holy Ghost is something great and unearthly, dissatisfied with the meagre conceptions of the many, yet not knowing where to look for what they need, are led to place the life of a Christian which 'is hid with Christ in God', in a sort of religious ecstasy, in a high-wrought sensibility on sacred subjects, in impassioned thoughts, an untrue tenderness of feeling, and an unnatural profession of all this in conversation. And further, from the same ignorance of the supernatural character of the Heavenly Gift, they attempt to measure it in each other by its sensible effects, and account none to be Christians but those whom they suppose they can ascertain to be such by their profession, language and carriage. On the other hand, sensible and soberminded men, offended at such excesses, acquiesce in the notion, that the gift of the Holy Ghost was almost peculiar to the Apostles' day, that now, at least, it does nothing more than make us decent and orderly members of society; the privileges bestowed upon us in Scripture being, as they conceive, but of an external nature, education and the like, or, at the most, a pardon of our sins and admission to God's favour, unaccompanied by any actual and inherent powers bestowed upon us. Such are the natural consequences of obscuring any of the doctrines which are revealed in mercy to our necessities.[2]

1. *P.S.*, III, p. 269

2. *P.S.*, III, pp. 267–9

True Christianity is the Presence of Persons—to know Christ and through Him, the Father. Obedience, not a frame of mind is the test: 'The whole duty and work of a Christian is made up of these two parts, Faith and Obedience; "looking unto Jesus", the Divine Object as well as Author of our faith, and acting according to His will.' Newman comments, 'I conceive that we are in danger, in this day, of insisting on neither of these as we might; regarding all true and careful consideration of the Object of faith, as barren orthodoxy, technical subtilty . . . making the test of our being religious, consist in our having what is called a spiritual state of heart'.[1] The Christian believes not simply in God, but in God as manifested in Christ, whom we must adore and love as our Redeemer and in the Holy Spirit, on whose gracious aids we depend. 'Frail man requires pardon and sanctification; can he do otherwise than devote himself to, and trust implicitly in his Redeemer and his Sanctifier? But if our Redeemer were not God, and our Sanctifier were not God, how great would have been our danger of preferring creatures to the Creator.' And Newman goes on to point out 'that this doctrine of the Trinity *is not proposed in Scripture as a mystery*'.[2] Revealed truth here is partial knowledge in a sphere where we are otherwise ignorant. Although we may be unable to answer all the objections that can be brought against a mystery, we are nonetheless able to accept it as true and to understand it. Many years later in the first part of *A Grammar of Assent*, Newman was still emphasising that in the life of religion the Blessed Trinity is not to be thought of as a mystery. The New Testament and the Liturgy bring home to us, as concrete realities, and in living images, that the Son is God and the Holy Spirit is God. 'Religion has to do with the real, and the real is the particular; theology has to do with what is notional, and the notional is the general and systematic.'[3]

'Evangelical theology', says Dean Church, 'had dwelt upon the work of Christ, and laid comparatively little stress on His example, or the picture left us of His Personality and Life. It regarded the Epistles of St Paul as the last word of the Gospel message.'

But now there was a change. 'The great Name stood no longer for an abstract symbol of doctrine, but for a Living Master, who could teach as well as save. . . . It was a change in the look and

1. *P.S.*, I, pp. 153–4 2. *P.S.*, I, pp. 80 and 210
3. *G.A.*, p. 140. Cf. below, p. 150

use of Scripture, which some can still look back to as an epoch in their religious history.'[1]

So we find Newman describing among the benefits of Christ's Coming,

> . . . that the Invisible God was then revealed in the form and history of man, revealed in those respects in which sinners most required to know Him, and nature spoke least distinctly, as a Holy yet Merciful Governor of His creatures. And thus the Gospels, which contain the memorials of this wonderful grace, are our principal treasures. They are (so to say) the text of revelation; and the Epistles, especially St Paul's, are as comments upon it, unfolding and illustrating it in its various parts, raising history into doctrine, ordinances into sacraments, detached words or actions into principles, and thus every where dutifully preaching His Person work and will. . . . He is the chief Prophet of the Church, and His Apostles do but explain His words and actions. . . . The like service is ministered to Him by the Creeds and doctrinal expositions of the early Church, which we retain in our services. They speak of no ideal being, such as the imagination alone contemplates, but of the very Son of God, whose life is recorded in the Gospels. Thus every part of the Dispensation tends to the manifestation of Him who is its centre.

This is the 'Salvation History' which the Holy Spirit has made known. 'The birth, the life, the death and resurrection of Christ, has been the text which He has illuminated. He has made history to be doctrine.'[2]

Also, Christ's Coming has made real and realisable the loving care of God for each individual:

> it is very difficult, in spite of the revelation made us in the Gospel, to master the idea of this particular providence of God. If we allow ourselves to float down the current of the world, living as other men, gathering up our notions of religion here and there, as it may be, we have little or no true comprehension of a particular Providence. We conceive that Almighty God works on a large plan; but we cannot realise the wonderful truth that He sees and thinks of individuals. We cannot believe He is really present every where, that He is wherever we are, though unseen. . . . We cannot bring ourselves to get fast hold of the solemn fact that He sees what is going on among ourselves at this moment; that this man falls and that man is exalted, at His silent, invisible appointment.

1. R. W. Church, *The Oxford Movement*, pp. 191–2
2. *P.S.*, II, pp. 155 and 227

This is brought home to us by our Lord:

The most winning property of our Saviour's mercy, (if it is right so to speak of it), is its dependence on time and place, person and circumstance; in other words its tender discrimination. It regards and consults for each individual as he comes before it. . . . This might be illustrated, as is often done, by our Lord's tender behaviour towards Lazarus and his sisters, or His tears over Jerusalem; or by His conduct towards St Peter. . . . But I will direct your attention rather to His treatment of the traitor Judas. . . .[1]

The first generations of the Church, needed no explicit declarations concerning His Sacred Person.' 'But when the light of His advent faded, and love waxed cold, then there was an opening for objection and discussion, and a difficulty in answering. Then doubts had to be allayed, questions set at rest, innovators silenced. Christians were forced to speak out against their will, lest heretics should speak instead of them.' Thus the Church has had to make her statement of Christian doctrine.

Another reason of these statements is as follows: time having proceeded, and the true traditions of Our Lord's ministry being lost to us, the Object of our faith is but faintly reflected on our minds, compared with the vivid picture presented before the early Christians . . . statements, such, for instance, as occur in the Te Deum and Athanasian Creed, are especially suitable in divine worship, inasmuch as they kindle and elevate the religious affections.[2]

Newman then lays down 'the Catholic doctrine of the Incarnation', and the pencil references to the Fathers in his volume of the sermons, already mentioned, are multiplied. There is this summary of Christ's work:

He bore to live in a world that slighted Him, for he lived in it, in order in due time to die for it. He came, as the appointed Priest, to offer sacrifice for those who took no part in the act of worship. . . . He died to rise again the third day, the Sun of Righteousness, fully displaying that splendour which had hitherto been concealed by the morning clouds. He rose again, to ascend to the right hand of God, there to plead His sacred wounds in token of our forgiveness.

After the Resurrection 'His Divine Essence streamed forth (so to say) on every side, and environed His Manhood, as in a cloud of glory'.[3]

1. *P.S.*, III, pp. 115–6, 120–1
2. *P.S.*, II, pp. 27–9
3. *P.S.*, II, pp. 39 and 143

Newman makes very clear in these sermons the central place in Christianity of the Paschal Mystery. Christ died for our sins and rose again for our salvation. Christ must depart in order to send the Spirit.

What are the deep and hidden reasons why Christ went and the Spirit came? Marvellous and glorious beyond our understanding! Let us worship in silence; meanwhile, let us jealously maintain this and every other portion of our Creed, lest, by dropping jot or tittle, we suffer truths concealed therein to escape us.

Newman was anxious to preach the Christian Faith in its purity, and thus here and throughout his sermons, he gives due emphasis to the primacy of Easter, and that at a time when among so many Christians its significance was overlooked.

We are able to see that the Saviour, when once He entered into this world, never so departed as to suffer things to be as they were before He came; for He is still with us, not in mere gifts, but by the substitution of His Spirit for Himself, and that, both in the Church, and in the souls of individual Christians.[1]

Following on the teaching about the Incarnation, Passion and the Risen Christ is a full doctrine of the Sacraments.

In truth, our Merciful Saviour has done much more for us than reveal the wonderful doctrines of the Gospel; He has enabled us to apply them . . . but how should we bring home His grace to ourselves? . . . how secure the comfortable assurance that He loves us personally, and will change our hearts, which we feel to be so earthly, and wash away our sins, which we confess to be so manifold, unless He had given us Sacraments,—means and pledges of grace,—keys which open the treasure-house of mercy. . . .

The Sacraments are instruments of the application of His merits to individual believers. Though He now sits on the right hand of God, He has, in one sense, never left the world since He first entered it; for by the ministration of the Holy Ghost, He is really with us in an unknown way, and ever imparts Himself to those who seek Him. . . . And as He is still with us, for all that He is in heaven, so, again, is the hour of His cross and passion ever mystically present, though it be past these eighteen hundred years. Time and space have no portion in the spiritual Kingdom, which He has founded; and the rites of His Church are as mysterious spells by which He annuls them. . . . Thus Christ shines through them, as through transparent bodies, without impediment. . . . He has touched them, and breathed upon them,

1. *P.S.*, II, pp. 213 and 221

when He ordained them; and thenceforth they have a virtue residing in them.[1]

From Hurrell Froude Newman had learned the doctrine of the Real Presence, and this Scriptural doctrine was developed in the Sermons.

We must not suppose that in leaving us He closed the gracious economy of His Incarnation . . . before He went away, He remembered our necessity, and completed His work, bequeathing to us a special mode of approaching Him, a Holy Mystery, in which we receive (we know not how,) the virtue of that Heavenly Body, which is the life of all that believe. This is the blessed Sacrament of the Eucharist, in which 'Christ is evidently set forth crucified among us;' that we, feasting upon the Sacrifice, may be 'partakers of the Divine Nature.' Let us give heed lest we be in the number of those, who 'discern not the Lord's Body,' and the 'exceeding great and precious promises' which are made to those who partake it.

Thus the Eucharist is a sacrifice and a meal. Newman continues:

Christ communicates life to us, one by one, by means of that holy and incorrupt nature which He assumed for our redemption. . . . Why should this communion with Him be thought incredible, mysterious and sacred as it is, when we know from the Gospels how marvellously He wrought, in the days of His humiliation, towards those who approached Him?[2]

Newman reminds his hearers that 'our chief ordinances are to be found' in Scripture, 'as the sacraments, public worship, the observance of the Lord's day, ordination, marriage and the like'.[3] Man's original debt is 'cancelled in Baptism, and all subsequent penalties respited by Absolution'.[4] Although Absolution was not the Anglican practice, he insisted that this power was intended to be conferred in the Anglican ordination service.

Newman had much to say, not only on sacraments, but on Common Worship and Liturgy. 'The services and ordinances of the Church are the outward form in which religion has been for ages represented to the world and has ever been known to us.'[5] He continually insisted on their importance, and on 25 March 1830 began Saints' Day Services at St Mary's.

1. *P.S.*, III, pp. 290–1, 277–8
2. *P.S.*, II, pp. 144–6
3. *P.S.*, II, p. 73
4. *P.S.*, III, p. 362
5. *P.S.*, II, p. 77

Can we devise a more powerful mode of preaching to men at large, and one in which the most unlearned and most timid among us might more easily partake, of preaching Christ as a warning and a remembrance, than if all who loved the Lord Jesus Christ in sincerity, made it a practice to throng the Churches on the week-day Festivals and various Holy Seasons . . .[1]

The Liturgy supports our faith: 'in the services of worship we elicit and realise the invisible'.[2] This is something more important than preaching, and, although Newman's sermons were so outstanding, he consistently taught people to think less of preaching than of what were invidiously called 'forms', the sacraments and services of the Church. Many of the sermons themselves are perfect models of what a liturgical homily, based on Holy Scripture, should be. But although Newman had a deep liturgical understanding, he was far removed from ritualism, and to the end of his Anglican days celebrated, as was customary, in surplice and hood.

It is abundantly clear what an exalted idea of the Church Newman had. It comes from Christ, it is the vehicle of His Spirit, and has charge of the Sacraments by which He reaches us. The 'Elect People of God . . . is but the Church of Christ under another name'. From the days when he was working as a curate in St Clement's, Newman had begun to grasp its true nature, as revealed in Scripture. He complains of those who 'have invented an Invisible Church, distinct and complete at present, and peopled by saints only,—as if Scripture said one word, anywhere, of a spiritual body existing in this world separate from, and independent of, the Visible Church'.[3]

It is allowable to speak of the Visible and Invisible Church, as two sides of one and the same thing, separated by our minds only, not in reality. . . . The Church of Christ, as Scripture teaches, is a visible body, invested with, or (I may say) existing in invisible privileges.[4]

Devotion to the Church is one of Newman's fundamental characteristics. Through it Revelation is preserved. In a sermon first preached in November 1829 he said:

If Christ has constituted one Holy Society (which He has done); if His Apostles have set it in order (which they did), and have expressly

1. *P.S.*, II, pp. 398–9
2. *P.S.*, III, p. 250
3. *P.S.*, III, p. 207
4. *P.S.*, III, pp. 221, 224

bidden us (as they have in Scripture) not to undo what they have begun; and if (in matter of fact) their Work so set in order and so blessed is among us to this very day (as it is), and we partakers of it, it were a traitor's act in us to abandon it. . . . We must transmit what we have received. We did not make the Church, we may not unmake it. As we believe it to be a Divine Ordinance, so we must ever protest against separation from it as a sin.[1]

But, alas, the Church is now divided:

You know time was when there was but one vast body of Christians, called the Church, throughout the world. It was found in every country where the name of Christ was named; it was everywhere governed in the same way by Bishops; it was everywhere descended from the Apostles through the line of those Bishops; and it was everywhere in perfect peace and unity together, branch with branch, all over the world. . . . But now all this beauty . . . is miserably defaced. That vast Catholic body, 'the Holy Church throughout the world', is broken into fragments by the power of the Devil; just as some huge barrier cliff which once boldly fronted the sea is at length cleft, parted, overthrown by the waves. Some portions of it are altogether gone, and those that remain are separated from each other. We are the English Catholics; abroad are the Roman Catholics, some of whom are among ourselves; elsewhere are the Greek Catholics, and so on. And thus we stand in this day of rebuke and blasphemy—clinging to our portion of the Ancient Rock which the waters are raging round and would fain overflow . . .[2]

From the time of Newman's conversion, long before he had any clear belief concerning the Church, the restoration of broken unity was one of his intentions in prayer. Among the prayers he wrote out and recited regularly was that dated 17 November 1817, during his first term at Oxford, when he was not yet seventeen. It was addressed to the Father:

Enlighten all by the Holy Spirit; turning all Jews, Musselmans and Pagans to Thee; converting all atheists and infidels, whether so in principle or practise; recovering all heretics from the error of their ways, and restoring all schismatics to Thy Holy Church; that there may be one fold and one shepherd . . .

Then there is a list of intentions drawn up in 1824–5. Intercession on Sunday was to be for the 'Universal Church of Christ —church of England—other Christian çhurches—for nominal

1. *P.S.*, III, p. 202 2. *P.S.*, III, pp. 191–2

Christians—for heretics, schismatics, papists etc,—for Jews, for Mohammedans—for heathens. . . .'

From Hurrell Froude Newman had also learned devotion to the Blessed Virgin. In a sermon in his second volume he wrote: 'Mary, His mother, was a sinner as others, and born of sinners; but she was set apart, "as a garden inclosed, a spring shut up, a fountain sealed", to yield a created nature to Him who was her Creator. . . . He, the Son of Mary, and she (if it may be said) the Mother of God.'[1] In a later sermon in the same volume preached on the Feast of the Annunciation 1832, he spoke of our Lady's holiness in a way that led him to be accused of holding the doctrine of the Immaculate Conception:

In her the destinies of the world were to be reversed, and the serpent's head bruised. On her was bestowed the greatest honour ever put upon any individual of our fallen race. . . .

But further, she is doubtless to be accounted blessed and favoured in herself, as well as in the benefits she has done us. Who can estimate the holiness and perfection of her, who was chosen to be the Mother of Christ? If to him that hath, more is given, and holiness and divine favour go together, (and this we are expressly told,) what must have been the angelic purity of her, whom the Creator Spirit condescended to overshadow with His miraculous presence? What must have been her gifts, who was chosen to be the only near earthly relative of the Son of God, the only one whom He was bound by nature to revere and look up to; the one appointed to train and educate Him, to instruct Him day by day, as He grew in wisdom and in stature? The contemplation runs to a higher subject, did we dare follow it; for what think you, was the sanctity and grace of that human nature, of which God formed his sinless Son; knowing as we do, 'that what is born of the flesh, is flesh'; and that 'none can bring forth a clean thing out of an unclean?' . . .

. . . For truly, she is raised above the condition of sinful beings, though she was a sinner; she is brought near to God, yet is but a creature. . . . We cannot combine in our thought of her, all we should ascribe with all we should withhold . . . for nothing is so calculated to impress on our minds that Christ is really partaker of our nature, and in all respects man, save sin only, as to associate Him with the thought of her, by whose ministration He became our brother.

. . . And when sorrow came upon her afterwards, it was but the blessed participation of her Son's sacred sorrows, not the sorrow of those who suffer for their sins.[2]

1. *P.S.*, II, p. 32

2. *P.S.*, II, pp. 128, 131–2, 135–7

Not content with this positive exposition of Revealed Religion, Newman also came forward to defend it against the attacks of unbelief and scepticism. During these early years up to the end of 1832, he preached a number of official University Sermons, which were not actually published in a volume for another decade. His views he developed more fully in the later *University Sermons* and in his *Grammar of Assent*, but as he explained at the end of his life:

> From the time that I began to occupy my mind with theological subjects I have been troubled at the prospect, which I considered to lie before us, of an intellectual movement against religion, so special as to have a claim upon the attention of all educated Christians.[1]

In the first of these early University Sermons he attempted to show that the true scientific spirit was 'first enjoined by the Gospel'. In subsequent sermons he appeals to conscience as 'the essential principle and sanction of religion in the mind'. It is the basis of natural religion and leads on to the idea of a personal God and to Christianity. Mere logical reasoning, though useful, is not necessary for faith. How many are really brought to belief by the logical arguments? An educated conscience 'seems to detect moral truth wherever it lies hid, and feels a conviction of its own accuracy which bystanders cannot account for; and this especially in the case of Revealed Religion, which is one comprehensive moral fact'. Those who follow conscience develop their characters in a way that influences others. Holiness and consistency seen in the concrete living person make him a light to those about him. 'A few highly-endowed men will rescue the world for centuries to come.' 'Revelation provides us with an important instrument for chastening and moulding our moral character.' It enlightens us only in proportion as we first submit to be darkened, whereas 'the so-called philosophical Christians' wish to 'be rid altogether of the shackles of a Revelation'.[2]

1. *Stray Essays on Controversial Points*, privately printed 1890, p. 104
2. *Fifteen Sermons Preached before the University of Oxford*, abbreviated as *U.S.*, pp. 18, 66, 97 and 172

CHAPTER 3

Leader of the Revival at Oxford (1833-8)

THE last words quoted in the previous chapter come from the University Sermon Newman preached on 2 December 1832, 'Wilfulness the Sin of Saul', and he concluded it by denouncing the general opposition of society to the Church, 'the irreverence towards Antiquity . . . the profanation of the Church, the bold transgression of the duty of Ecclesiastical Unity, the avowed disdain of what is called party religion (though Christ undeniably made a party the vehicle of His doctrine, and did not cast it at random on the world, as men would now have it,) the growing indifference to the Catholic Creed, the sceptical objections' and so on.[1] While Newman was recovering the Catholic Creed in Protestant England, the attacks on it and on the Church of England were increasing. 'Great events,' Newman explains in the *Apologia*, 'were happening at home and abroad, which brought out into form and passionate expression the various beliefs which had so gradually been winning their way into my mind'.[2] In France there had been a revolution which had driven out the King and the clericals: in England, Parliament, which controlled the Church, had been thrown open to men of all beliefs. The Reform Bill had been passed, and it was generally agreed that the new Whig government must now reform the Church. The Bishops were unpopular on account of their resistance to the Reform Bill, and, in any case, like nearly all Englishmen, were not prepared to regard the Church as independent of the State. There were many proposals as to how the State should renovate the Church, even to making it 'a kind of gigantic mechanics' institute', and proposals, too, that it should modify the Creed, that is, loosen the hold on revealed truth. The Evangelical party, still growing in influence, had not much use either for the Church or for the Creeds, and thus, as Newman thought, played into the

1. *U.S.*, p. 174 2. *Apo.*, p. 30

hands of Liberals and secularists. He wrote a little later to his aunt, Elizabeth Newman:

The most religiously-minded men are ready to give up important doctrinal truths because they do not *understand their value*. A cry is raised that the Creeds are unnecessarily minute, and even those who would defend them, through ignorance cannot. . . . What is most painful is that the clergy are so utterly ignorant on the subject. We have no *theological* education, and instead of profiting by the example of past times, we attempt to decide the most intricate questions, whether of doctrine or conduct, by our blind and erring reason.[1]

The wide circle of doctrine he had recovered was threatened not only by the spirit of the age, but by the immediate turn of events.

For the time being, however, the day after preaching on 'Wilfulness the Sin of Saul', Newman left the scene of his activity. He was exhausted by writing his book *The Arians of the Fourth Century*, his supply of pupils, cut off by the Provost, Hawkins, at Oriel, had come to an end, and he gladly accepted the invitation of Hurrell Froude and his father Archdeacon Froude to go on a tour of the Mediterranean. They sailed at once from Falmouth in the *Hermes*, a steamship of 600 tons. The winter was spent in visiting Malta, Corfu, Greece, Rome and Naples. Newman was fascinated by the beauty, and also, thanks to his knowledge of the Greek and Latin classics, by the historical memories of the places he visited. Undoubtedly his mind was broadened, but it must not be forgotten that he was preoccupied during his travels by the situation in England. Nor must it be forgotten how broad the mind of this clerical don already was. His interests were wide. He had studied not only the classics and theology, but mathematics, geology and literature. He was a practised musician who loved to play the violin, and when he read Wellington's despatches they made him 'burn to be a soldier'. At Oriel and in his own family, in the person of his brother Charles, he came into practical contact with unbelief and scepticism. Through his family too, he knew all the difficulties of keeping house on an inadequate income. During his travels there was plenty of scope for his wide-ranging interests, but all the while he was haunted by the thought of the struggle in England and the success of the Liberals there: 'England was in my thoughts solely.'[2] At Rome he and Froude called on Nicholas

1. *Letters and Correspondence of John Henry Newman during his life in the English Church*, edited by Anne Mozley, II, pp. 129–30
2. *Apo.*, p. 33

Wiseman, at that time Rector of the English College. When the latter expressed a wish that they might visit Rome a second time, Newman replied gravely, 'We have a work to do in England'.

He found an outlet for his feelings in the poetry he wrote during his tour, some of it quite 'fierce' in its tone. The flow of verse began in the middle of November 1832, as his Oxford labours were ending. 'England' was written just after leaving Gibraltar:

> Tyre of the West, and glorying in thy name
>   More than in Faith's pure flame!
> O trust not crafty fort nor rock renown'd
>   Earn'd upon hostile ground;
> Wielding Trade's master-keys, at thy proud will
> To lock or loose its waters, England! trust not still.[1]

At Rome, in April he described his sense of vocation, in 'Our Future', on the text 'What I do, thou knowest not now; but thou shalt know hereafter'. The poem was written at Tre Fontane, where St Paul was martyred:

> Did we but see,
> When life first open'd, how our journey lay
> Between its earliest and its closing day,
>   Or view ourselves, as we one time shall be,
> Who strive for the high prize, such sight would break
> The youthful spirit, though bold for Jesu's sake.
>
> But Thou, dear Lord!
> Whilst I traced out bright scenes which were to come,
> Isaac's pure blessings, and a verdant home,
>   Didst spare me, and withhold Thy fearful word;
> Wiling me year by year, till I am found
> A pilgrim pale, with Paul's sad girdle bound.[2]

Nevertheless, in April 1833, when the Froudes returned to England, Newman decided to revisit Sicily, having been quite taken by its beauty in the glimpse he had had of it. To his sister Jemima he wrote, 'Spring in Sicily! It is the nearest approach to Paradise of which sinful man is capable'. There he fell ill of typhoid fever, but was confident he would not die, and told the manservant who accompanied and cared for him, that 'I thought God had some work for me'. Newman came to regard it as a

1. *Verses on Various Occasions*, p. 89

2. *Op. cit.*, p. 133

purifying illness, preparing him for his mission in England. On the way home, when his ship lay becalmed in the Straits between Corsica and Sardinia, he wrote 'Lead kindly Light'. He wanted to be guided by God's providence:

> The distant scene—one step enough for me . . .
> . . . I loved to choose and see my path, but now
> Lead Thou me on!

The bulk of Newman's poetry was written between November 1832, just as he was about to leave England, and his return, the following summer. It shows how full he was of the evils threatening the Church, and the harsh necessity of reforming it. His tone is very different from that of the gentle verse of Keble in the *Christian Year*. Newman is forceful and fierce and tormented, but with an underlying security—God's providence will enable him to fulfil His tasks, in spite of his weakness. These poems, written, like most of the sermons already mentioned, before the official start of the Oxford Movement, were published in the *British Magazine*, and then collected to form the greater part of the *Lyra Apostolica*, to which Keble, Froude and others also contributed, and which was published in 1836.

Newman reached his mother's house near Littlemore on 9 July 1833, on the same day as his brother Frank, still an Evangelical, returned after a long absence on a fruitless missionary journey to Persia. Within a week, on 14 July, Keble came to Oxford, and preached from the pulpit at St Mary's the Assize Sermon on 'National Apostasy', which Newman, playing down his own work before and after that date, called the beginning of the Oxford Movement. The immediate occasion of Keble's protest was the abolition by Parliament of a number of unneeded Protestant bishoprics in Catholic Ireland. Thus was the State interfering with the successors of the apostles. In the preface he printed to his Assize sermon, a week later, Keble asked how true Anglicans were to 'continue their communion with the Church *established*, (hitherto the pride and comfort of their lives,) without any taint of those Erastian Principles on which she is now avowedly to be governed? What answer can we make henceforth to the partisans of the Bishop of Rome, when they taunt us with being a mere Parliamentary Church? And how, consistently with our present relations to *the State*, can even the doctrinal purity and integrity of the MOST SACRED ORDER be preserved?'[1] The Oxford Movement began by reasserting the independence of the Church, as a society deriving its authority from the Apostles. Only if this principle came to be widely accepted would the Church be in a position to resist the claim of the State to regulate her affairs, and be able to preserve the revealed truths of which she was the guardian. There was an excellent case for suppressing Irish bishoprics, but their abolition by Parliament involved a principle, and thus became the occasion, soon forgotten, of a much deeper religious movement. Doctrine would be sacrificed to expedience, if the Church was the slave of the State. The small group of anti-Erastian High Churchmen now bestirred itself. One meeting, attended by Hurrell Froude and William Palmer of Worcester College, but not by Newman, was held at Hadleigh in Suffolk. The establishment was there proposed of committees to spread Catholic principles among Churchmen, and to organise a petition to the Archbishop of Canterbury. Newman felt convinced that more energetic methods were required. Men who knew and understood each other should work together. 'Living movements do not come of committees.'[2] He suggested to Keble and Froude an informal association to publish tracts. He himself wrote four during August, and printed them. Keble and Froude gave him their support. These *Tracts for the Times* were short clarion calls, in defence of the Church's independence. The very first proclaimed the doctrine of the apostolic succession. By the end of the year, twenty *Tracts* had appeared, eleven written by Newman himself. During the autumn he rode about the country from parsonage to parsonage distributing parcels of them. They were soon selling in large numbers. Newman, with only his duties as Vicar of St Mary's, was able to devote his energies to the movement that was now under weigh. He insisted, 'We have no concern with politics. We have nothing to do with maintaining the temporalities of the Church'.[3] He attended meetings and gatherings of all kinds, dinners, soirées, and carried on a large correspondence. He husbanded his time, met people and discussed business at meals, and thus was able to continue assiduously with his patristic studies. On 23 April 1834,

1. John Keble, *National Apostasy*, p. iv, *Sermons Academical, and Occasional*, Oxford 1848, p. 128
2. *Apo.*, p. 39
3. *Letters and Correspondence of John Henry Newman during his Life in the English Church*, edited by Anne Mozley, II, p. 4

in addition to the regular sermons, he began a weekly lecture in Adam de Brome's Chapel in St Mary's, on the idea of the Church, and on 30 June he began the daily service there, in the chancel. The first volume of *Parochial Sermons* was published on 11 March 1834, the second a year later, and Newman's name began to be known beyond Oxford circles.

At the same time the liberal attack on the University of Oxford, which was still the 'sacred city of Anglicanism', began. Its immediate protagonist was the broad churchman, Renn Dickson Hampden, who became a Fellow of Oriel in 1814, and was now principal of St Mary's Hall. In 1832 he had published his Bampton Lectures on *The Scholastic Philosophy, considered in its relation to Christian Theology*, in which he watered down the dogmatic element, the revealed truth in Christianity. At the end of 1834 he sent Newman his pamphlet urging the abolition of religious tests and the admission of others than Anglicans to the University. Those who looked on the Established Church simply as the true Christian Church in England and Christianity as the law of the land, were thoroughly opposed to this proposal, but what horrified Newman far more was the argument used in Hampden's pamphlet. He made a distinction between 'the simple religion of Christ' and theological opinion, in which he included the Trinitarian doctrine, and maintained that the Church of England was not dogmatic in its spirit. As Newman tells us in the *Apologia* 'my battle was with liberalism; by liberalism I mean the anti-dogmatic principle and its developments. . . . From the age of fifteen, dogma has been the fundamental principle of my religion: I know no other religion. . . . As well can there be filial love without the fact of a father, as devotion without the fact of a Supreme Being'.[1] The proposal to allow non-Anglicans to enter the University was defeated, thanks largely to the general rallying of Churchmen which the Oxford Movement had set on foot. Barely a year later, in February 1836, Hampden was appointed Regius Professor of Divinity at Oxford, to the fury of the Tractarians, and indeed of the believing Evangelicals and also the old-fashioned High Churchmen. Tempers rose, but Lord Melbourne, the Prime Minister, insisted that the appointment must stand. In the end all that the Convocation of the University could do was to pass a kind of censure on Hampden. This it did in May, by 474 votes to 94. Newman, by

1. *Apo.*, pp. 48–9

his pamphlet, *Elucidations of Dr Hampden's Theological Statements*, took a leading part in the fray, but the opposition to Hampden's appointment was very far from being confined to the Tractarians. It was widely agreed at Oxford that Hampden's views undermined the Christian faith.

Partly owing to his absence from Oxford and partly owing to illness, Pusey did not at first take an active part in the Tractarian movement. At the of 1833, however, he wrote 'Thoughts on the Benefits of the System of Fasting, enjoined by our Church', which became *Tract 18*. The *Tracts* had until then been unsigned, and to show that he was not entirely committed, Pusey now added his initials. This had an effect contrary to what he intended, and gave the movement the prestige of his name. He had been Regius Professor of Hebrew and Canon of Christ Church since 1828, and was known for his learning and piety. The *Tracts* soon changed their form and developed into small treatises.

Meanwhile, Hurrell Froude, who had done so much to encourage Newman in his Catholic views, was dying of consumption. In the autumn of 1835 Newman visited him for the last time at Dartington Parsonage in Devon, the home of Archdeacon Froude. Hurrell Froude died on 28 February 1836. That year marked the end of the first period of the Oxford Movement, and was a milestone in Newman's life. In May his mother died, and in the course of the year his two surviving sisters were married to two brothers, Harriett to Tom, and Jemima to John Mozley. Thus his family was no longer available to care for the poor people at Littlemore, but their church, now finished, was dedicated on 23 September 1836. After Hurrell Froude's death Newman was given his set of the Roman Breviary, and began to recite it daily, omitting, however, such things as prayers directly invoking our Lady, which were against the teaching and practice of the Church of England.

Newman could not help being astonished at the success of the Tractarian movement. Looking back, shortly after he had left the Church of England, he wrote:

From beginnings so small, from elements of thought so fortuitous, with prospects so unpromising, the Anglo-Catholic party suddenly became a power in the National Church, and an object of alarm to her rulers and friends. Its originators would have found it difficult to say what they aimed at of a practical kind: rather they put forth views and principles for their own sake, because they were true, as if they were obliged to say them; and, as they might be themselves surprised at their earnestness in uttering them, they had as great cause to be surprised at the success which attended their propagation. . . . In a very few years a school of opinion was formed, fixed in its principles, indefinite and progressive in their range; and it extended itself into every part of the country. . . . And so it proceeded, getting stronger and stronger every year, till it came into collision with the Nation, and that Church of the Nation, which it began by professing especially to serve.[1]

In reviving the full circle of Christian truths, Newman appeared to be spreading the teaching of the Church of Rome. There could be no more damaging accusation in Protestant England. Quite early on, Bowden wrote to Newman from London, 'the world accuses you of popery'. To Newman, who considered that he was preaching the New Testament Revelation, the accusation appeared quite gratuitous. Indeed he still thought that the Roman Church was linked with Antichrist. In *Tract 15* he expressed the belief that at the time of the Council of Trent 'it is to be feared the whole Roman Communion bound itself, by a perpetual bond and covenant, to the cause of Antichrist', and in *Tract 20*, 'Their communion is infected with heresy; we are bound to flee it as a pestilence'. Elsewhere he complained of the cruelty of the Roman Church 'in its unsparing sacrifice of the happiness and virtue of individuals to a phantom of public expediency', and of its 'intense hatred of us, and the iron temper with which she resists all proposals for ever so little concession'. He complained of her 'lying wonders', statues of our Lady, masses without communicants. 'In her mass the priest prays and offers instead of the people, not for and with them.'[2] Yet she was the Mother of the English Church, and was deceived, rather than being a deceiver, for otherwise there would be no apostolic succession, the line of the apostles would have been lost.[3] In *The Arians of the Fourth Century*, Newman had written, 'The grant of permanency was made in the beginning, not to the mere doctrine of the Gospel, but to the Association itself built upon the doctrine,' and he then referred to the Petrine text, Matthew 16: 'Thus the Ecclesiastical Body is

1. *Apo.*, p. 76, *Diff.*, I, p. 96
2. 'Home Thoughts from Abroad' in the *British Magazine*, (Feb. 1834), pp. 123 and 129. Cf. *The Via Media, of the Anglican Church*, abbreviated as *V.M.*, II, p. 429
3. 'How to accomplish it,' *Discussions and Arguments*, pp. 4–6

a divinely appointed means, towards realising the great evangelical blessings.'[1]

In view of Bowden's warning, Newman devoted three *Tracts*, 38, 40 and 71, to the Roman question. 'The glory of the English Church is that it has taken the *Via Media*, as it has been called. It lies *between* the (so called) Reformers and the Romanists.' The English Church was not set up at the Reformation. It holds 'the doctrines which the Apostles spoke in Scripture and impressed upon the early Church'. But it has fallen away from its principles and is in need of a second reformation. Thus it appears 'that the members of the English Church of the present day differ from the principles of the Church of Rome more than our forefathers differed'.[2] There was a danger that people whose devotional feelings were not satisfied in the Church of England would go to Rome, but truth must come before holiness. As long as Rome taught error there could be no union with her. The errors Newman mentioned were chiefly practical ones, ideas about the Mass, the refusal of the cup to the laity, compulsory confession, Indulgences, Purgatory, the invocation of saints, images.[3]

Newman determined to clarify his ideas on the Church and did so by lecturing on the subject in St Mary's from 1834 to 1836. The result was a book, *Lectures on the Prophetical Office of the Church viewed relatively to Romanism and Popular Protestantism*, published in 1837. If he was writing controversy, his aim was ecumenical. In the preface he quoted from the seventeenth-century Anglican theologian, John Bramhall,

> My desire hath been to have Truth for my chiefest friend, and no enemy but error. If I have had any bias, it hath been my desire for peace, which our common Saviour left as a legacy to His Church, that I might live to see the re-union of Christendom, for which I shall always bow the knees of my heart to the Father of our Lord Jesus Christ. It is not impossible that this desire of unity may have produced some unwilling error of love, but certainly I am most free from the wilful love of error.[4]

Guarded by the Anglican divines, Newman wished to show from the ancient sources that a visible Church was an essential part of the Christian faith, the principle of true Catholicism, which

1. *Ari.*, p. 258
2. *V.M.*, II, pp. 28, 31, 24
3. *V.M.*, II, pp. 106–12
4. *V.M.*, I, pp. xii–xiii

Protestants denied and Catholics perverted. The Church of England took the middle road, the *Via Media*. She held that the one visible Church had split into three branches, Greek, Roman and Anglican, and that revealed truth was to be found in its integrity before the split, in the teaching of antiquity, in Scripture and the Fathers. Protestantism, with its emphasis on private judgment, rejected the idea of this authority. Popery, which held that the present-day Church was infallible, and justified its beliefs and practices by an appeal to its own teaching, also rejected it. Newman admitted that to some extent the Papists also appealed to antiquity, but their doctrine of infallibility led them to neglect it in practice. 'Romanism,' he maintained, 'by its pretence of infallibility, lowers the standard and quality of Gospel obedience, as well as impairs its mysterious and sacred character; and this in various ways. When religion is reduced in all its parts to a system, there is a hazard of something earthly being made the chief object of our contemplation instead of our Maker . . . [Romanism] provides us with a sort of graduated scale of devotion and obedience, and engrosses our thoughts with the details of a mere system, to a comparative forgetfulness of its professed Author.' When Newman republished his *Lectures* as a Catholic in 1878, he commented: 'There is a certain truth in this remark, but a man must have a large knowledge of Catholics and of the effect of their system upon them, to assert with confidence what is here imagined of them.'[1] Newman never forgot that Christianity is the Presence of Persons. Besides this moral objection, there was the political one against the Roman Church, 'if she stunts or distorts the growth of the soul in spiritual excellence, it is because . . . she has in view political objects, visible fruits, temporal expediency'. Again Newman commented in 1878, at the end of the reign of Pius IX, that the Church, being a visible body, was in a sense a political power. Politics are absorbing, 'it is not wonderful then that grave scandals from time to time occur among those who constitute its executive, or legislative, from their being led off from spiritual aims by secular. These scandals hide from the world for a while, and from large classes and various ranks of society, for long intervals, the real sanctity, beauty and persuasiveness of the Church and her children.'[2]

If Newman found it necessary later to clarify the objections he

1. *V.M.*, I, p. 102 2. *V.M.*, I, pp. 106–7

made to Roman infallibility, he found little to disavow of the lectures devoted to the appeal to Christian antiquity, which are the ones of ecumenical value today. The appeal to Scripture and antiquity has been the means of drawing Anglicans and Catholics together. It is an authority both accept, but eventually Newman came to the conclusion that it was not self-sufficing. In the 1878 edition of his *Lectures* he remarked that 'Revelation is the initial and essential idea of Christianity', but 'history and the patristical writings do not absolutely decide the truth or falsehood of all important theological propositions, any more than Scripture decides it. . . . They make a doctrine more or less probable, but rarely contain a statement, or suggest a conclusion, which cannot be plausibly evaded. The definition of the Church is commonly needed to supply the defects of logic'.[1] Yet Newman was very clear that this infallible power—the existence of which he admitted after he became a Catholic—was limited by the very content of the revealed truth it claimed to clarify and impose. As an Anglican he maintained that revealed truth was unimpaired only before unity had been broken. Yet he always claimed a certain infallibility for the Church even as an Anglican, writing in the *Lectures*, 'Not only is the Church Catholic bound to teach the Truth, but she is ever divinely guided to teach it. . . . She is indefectible in it, and therefore not only has authority to enforce, but is of authority in declaring it'.[2] On the other hand, the Church was not a judge. 'She bears witness to a fact, that such and such a doctrine, or such a sense of Scripture, has ever been received and came from the Apostles; the proof of this lies in her own unanimity throughout her various branches, next in the writings of the Ancient Fathers; and she acts upon this her witness as the executive does in civil matters, and is responsible for it; but she does not undertake of herself to determine the sense of Scripture, she has no immediate power over it, she but alleges and submits to what is ancient and Catholic. The mere Protestant, indeed, and the Romanist may use Antiquity,' but they use it simply as material for their own judgments. 'We, on the contrary, consider Antiquity and Catholicity to be the real guides, and the Church their organ.' In a note to the Catholic edition of the *Lectures* in 1878, Newman asked, 'How can history, that is, words and deeds which are dead

1. *V.M.*, I, pp. xlvii and 38
2. *V.M.*, I, p. 190

and gone, act as an effectual living decider of quarrels between living men?'[1]

For the moment, however, there was Newman's theory of the *Via Media*. It seemed, nevertheless, to labour under one great difficulty, as he pointed out in the Introductory Lecture, 'it had no exact counterpart in early times'.

Protestantism and Popery are real religions; no one can doubt about them; they have furnished the mould in which nations have been cast: but the *Via Media* has never existed except on paper, it has never been reduced to practice . . . it still remains to be tried whether what is called Anglicanism, the religion of Andrewes, Laud, Hammond, Butler, and Wilson is capable of being professed, acted on, and maintained on a large sphere of action and through a sufficient period.[2]

Newman and his friends devoted all their energies to removing this reproach.

1. *V.M.*, p. 269 2. *V.M.*, I, pp. 16–17

CHAPTER 4

Newman's Influence at its Height

SIR MOUNSTUART E. GRANT DUFF, in *Notes from a Diary*, describes a dinner party at which he was present on 13 March 1879.

The conversation turning upon Newman, Gladstone said: 'I do not believe that there has been anything like his influence in Oxford, when it was at its height, since Abelard lectured in Paris. I myself, in my undergraduate days, saw just the commencement of it. It was beginning to be the custom to go and hear him on Sunday afternoon at St Mary's.'[1]

Gladstone left Oxford in January 1832, after taking his degree, and as we have seen, Newman left it at the end of the same year to embark upon his Mediterranean tour. We have also seen what his teaching was at that period, before the beginning of the Oxford Movement. After 1836 comes the second period of the Movement, when Newman's influence was, as Gladstone put it, at its height. Newman said the same in the *Apologia*:

In the spring of 1839 my position in the Anglican Church was at its height. I had supreme confidence in my controversial *status*, and I had a great and still growing success in recommending it to others.[2]

It was a period of intense activity. In 1837 he began the early Communion Service at St Mary's and was lecturing twice a week there, during the season, in addition to his constant preaching. At this time that judge of men, the old President of Magdalen, Martin Routh, who always spoke of 'the great Newman', remarked of him, different from so many of his contemporaries, 'I am sure he is not looking to get on in life,' and the youthful James Anthony Froude noticed that his face was 'remarkably like that of Julius Caesar', and he added, 'I have often thought of the resemblance,

1. *Notes from a Diary, 1873–1881*, London 1898, II, p. 121
2. *Apo.*, p. 93

and believed that it extended to the temperament'.[1] The likeness is noticeable still in the bust by Westmacott.

Newman had a remarkable mission, the revival of so much of the Revealed Religion of Christianity. 'I held a large bold system of religion, very unlike the Protestantism of the day.'[2] His high ethical standard, which formed so important a part of the attraction he exercised, was derived from the doctrines he preached.

Again it is only by specimens and quotations that we can penetrate into the secret of his influence, and appreciate how it was that he induced so many people to embark upon real spiritual lives. He elaborated the Christian truths, not like a theologian in his lecture hall or his study, but as a pastor who wished his hearers and readers to build their Christian lives on the foundations laid in the New Testament. He wished to provide for them a complete and balanced doctrine, derived from Scripture and the Fathers. His teaching was welcomed by many in the Church of England, where it has continued to be held in high honour. It has also been received with ever increasing appreciation in the Church of Rome. The late Abbot Vonier used to sigh for a classical theology, where every truth of revelation would be stated in its proper proportion and balance, and not, as is so often inevitable, distorted, or exaggerated, or obscured by reaction against heresy. Needless to say, it is impossible for anyone to work out the doctrines of Christianity, from the sources, completely *in vacuo*. All the same, Newman was in a strikingly privileged position. Unlike the Roman theologians, he was brought up under the influence of no dominant philosophy or tradition of theology. If he made use of the seventeenth-century Anglican divines, it was, as he confessed, rather to protect and defend what he had elaborated independently from Holy Scripture and the Fathers. If he reacted against heresy, it was against the general heresy which rejected Revealed Religion. And so it comes about that, especially in these later Anglican writings, we find a classical, a truly Catholic Catholicism.

Another opinion of Gladstone's in 1879 was given in reply to the question 'which of Newman's writings will be read in a hundred years?' 'I think all his parochial sermons will be read.'[3]

1. 'The Oxford Counter-Reformation,' in *Short Studies on Great Subjects*, London 1907, V., p. 197
2. *Apo.*, p. 93
3. *Notes from a Diary, 1873–1881*, p. 140

The first three volumes of parochial sermons, which represent Newman's preaching up to the end of 1835, most of them first delivered before the end of 1832, have already been dealt with. After this there was a pause, and the next three volumes were not published until 1839, 1840 and early in 1842. Almost all the sermons in these later volumes were preached between 1836 and 1841. There have been many graphic descriptions of Newman's sermons in St Mary's. Dean Church's verdict was, 'They made men think of the things which the preacher spoke of, and not of the sermon or the preacher'.[1] The influence of sermons and lectures was greater still, when they appeared in print. That, at least, was Newman's view in a letter of 1849: 'I *do* think that my influence among persons who have *not* seen me has been indefinitely greater than among those who have.'[2] The sermon volumes were read eagerly, all over the English-speaking world. There was an appetite for printed sermons in those days, but they did not usually go through more than one edition of a thousand copies. Newman's volumes of parochial sermons went through five, four and three large editions, only his sixth volume in 1842 being limited to two editions, owing to his leaving the Church of England in 1845. It was through the published sermons that his teaching and influence were spread. Along with Newman's later sermon volumes must be included *Lectures on the Doctrine of Justification*, first delivered in Adam de Brome's Chapel in St Mary's during 1837, and published in March 1838.

The pre-Tractarian High Churchman, W. F. Hook, Vicar of Leeds, bears testimony to the effect of Newman's printed word. To him Hook wrote on 27 March 1841: 'For my part I am under the very deepest obligations to you. Your sermons have done me more good than almost any work: and your work on Justification has opened to me, now I have studied it, a field for thought, on which I hope to profit to my dying day.'[3] Twenty years later, a greater authority, J. J. Döllinger, wrote to Newman that he had read *Lectures on the Doctrine of Justification* twice, and that it 'is in my estimation one of the best theological books published in

1. R. W. Church, *The Oxford Movement*, p. 130
2. *The Letters and Diaries of John Henry Newman*, edited by Charles Stephen Dessain and others, abbreviated as *L. and D.*, XIII, p. 99
3. W. R. W. Stephens, *The Life and Letters of Walter Farquhar Hook*, London 1880, II, p. 67

this century'.[1] Newman's aim in writing this work was irenical and ecumenical. He wished to show that the teaching of Roman Catholic theologians on God's gift of grace to men, and that of all Protestants (except those extreme Evangelicals who held a rigid doctrine of justification by faith only), could be reconciled. He thought that this could be done by presenting revealed truth in fullness and balance, and the teaching he now elaborated as an Anglican, he still held to, when he republished his *Lectures* in 1874. In the Advertisement to the original edition he explained his purpose.

The present Volume originated in the following way: It was brought home to the writer from various quarters, that a suspicion existed in many serious minds against certain essential Christian truths, such as Baptismal Regeneration and the Apostolical Ministry, under the impression that they fostered notions of human merit, were prejudicial to the inward life of religion, and incompatible with the doctrine of justifying faith . . .[2]

Newman wished to reconcile the Lutheran view that it is faith which makes men pleasing to God, and that of 'the Romanists that justification consists in spiritual renovation'. Neither of these explanations was adequate.

When Faith is said to be the inward principle of acceptance, the question rises, what gives to faith its acceptableness? . . . faith is acceptable as having something in it, which unbelief has not; that something, what is it? It must be God's grace, if God's grace act *in* the soul, and not merely externally, as in the way of Providence. If it acts in us, and has a presence in us, when we have faith, then the having that grace or that presence, and not faith, which is its result, must be the real token, the real state of a justified man.

On the other hand:

. . . if we say that justification consists in a supernatural quality imparted to the soul by God's grace, as the Romanists say, then, in like manner, the question arises, is this quality all that is in us of heaven? does not the grace itself, as an immediate divine power or presence, dwell in the hearts which are gifted with this renovating principle?

If so:

1. *Ward*, I, p. 444
2. *Lectures on the Doctrine of Justification*, abbreviated as *Jfc.*, p. v. Again, the quotations are from the first edition, and the references to the uniform edition

. . . then surely its possession is really our justification, and not renewal or the principle of renewal.

And thus by tracing back further the lines of thought on which these apparently discordant views are placed, they are made to converge; they converge, that is, supposing there to be vouchsafed to us, an inward divine presence, of which both faith and spiritual renovation are fruits.[1]

Newman shows from the New Testament that what is there promised to men is not merely a quality of mind, but an inward Gift, and he reaches the triumphant conclusion: '*This* is to be justified, to receive the Divine Presence within us, and be made a Temple of the Holy Ghost.' Newman adds:

If this notion of the literal indwelling of God within us, whether in the way of nature or of grace, be decried as a sort of mysticism, I ask, in reply, whether it can possibly be but that His presence is in us, if He is every where; and whether the same tone of reasoning which denies that it is, does not also tend to deny the doctrine of His literal Omnipresence? So much in behalf of the general doctrine of God's presence in all His works. And if He is every where and dwells in all, there is no antecedent objection against taking Scripture literally, no difficulty in supposing that the truth is as Scripture says,—that as He dwells in us in one mode in the way of nature, so He is in us in another in the way of grace . . .[2]

After further proof from the New Testament of the Divine Indwelling, Newman concludes that

. . . Christ's sacred Presence, which shines forth in the heart straight upon the word of justification, creates a renewal there as certainly as a light involves illumination, or fire heat. And on the other hand, since quenching this renovating Presence necessarily leads to its departure, renewal may be considered the condition on our part as well as the result of justification. The first gift runs into the second as its necessary limit: and the second being rejected, carries away with it the first. And the one cannot be separated from the other except in idea, unless the sun's rays can be separated from the sun, or the power of purifying from water.[3]

These quotations bring home the mastery of his great subject which Newman had acquired, and similarly, if we want to trace the difference between the earlier and later volumes of *Parochial*

1. *Jfc.*, pp. 134, 136–7 2. *Jfc.*, pp. 144–5 3. *Jfc.*, p. 154

Sermons we must point to the greater mastery and completeness. It is substantially the same teaching, the same concrete 'personalism', the same psychological insight into other minds, but now more confident, with more experience behind it. It is English Christianity at its noblest, for Newman preaches not a theory or philosophy of his own, but the Christian Revelation: not Christian doctrine in the abstract, but the truths of faith as bringing us into new and close relations with God. He had a horror of 'unreal words' and professions. 'To make professions is to play with edged tools.' 'It is not easy to learn that new language which Christ has brought us.' 'Aim at things and your words will be right without aiming.' 'That a thing is true, is no reason that it should be said, but that it should be done; that it should be acted upon; that it should be made our own inwardly.'[1]

The first thing was to bring men to *realise* the unseen world.

We are born into a world of sense; that is, of real things which lie around us.... They act upon us and we know it; and we act upon them in turn and know we do.

But all this does not interfere with the existence of that other world which I speak of, acting upon us, yet not impressing us with the consciousness that it does so. It may as really be present and exert an influence as that which reveals itself to us. And that such a world there is, Scripture tells us. Do you ask what it is, and what it contains? I will not say that all that belongs to it is vastly more important than what we see, for among things visible are our fellow-men, and nothing created is more precious and noble than a human soul. But still, taking the things which we see altogether, and the things we do not see altogether, the world we do not see is on the whole a much higher world than that which we do see. For, first of all, He is there who is above all beings, who has created all, before whom they are all as nothing, and with whom nothing can be compared. . . . It appears, then, that the things which are seen are but a part, and but a secondary part of the beings about us. Once, and once only, for thirty three years has He condescended to become one of the beings that are seen, when, in the Person of His Only-begotten Son, He was, by an unspeakable mercy, born of the Virgin Mary into this sensible world.[2]

After the sense of the unseen world, comes another fundamental theme, that runs through all Newman's preaching and thought—his sense of the loving Providence of God.

1. *P.S.*, V, pp. 33, 44–5 2. *P.S.*, IV, pp. 201–3

Let a person, who trusts he is on the whole serving God acceptably, look back upon his past life, and he will find how critical were moments and acts, which at the time seemed the most indifferent: as for instance the school he was sent to as a child, the occasion of his falling in with those persons who have most benefited him, the accidents which determined his calling or his prospects, whatever they were. God's hand is ever over His own, and He leads them forward by a way they know not of.[1]

Then Newman emphasises our dependence on God. He has made us for Himself:

We need to escape from ourselves to something beyond; and much as we may wish it otherwise, and may try to make idols of ourselves, nothing short of God's presence is our true refuge; every thing else is either a mockery, or but an expedient useful for its season or in its measure.

How miserable then is he, who does not practically know this great truth! . . . He fancies he can live without an object. He fancies that he is sufficient for himself. . . . You see the educated man, full of thought, full of intelligence, full of action, but with a stone heart, as cold and dead as regards his affections, as if he were the poor ignorant country-men. You see others, with warm affections, perhaps, for their families, with benevolent feelings towards their fellow-men, yet stopping there; centering their hearts on what is sure to fail them, as being perishable; Life passes, riches fly away, popularity is fickle, the senses decay, the world changes, friends die. One alone is constant; One alone is true to us; One alone can be all things to us.[2]

Newman is led on to explain that:

. . . the thought of God, and nothing short of it, is the happiness of man; for though there is much besides to serve as subject of knowledge or motive for action, or instrument of excitement, yet the affections require a something more vast and more enduring than anything created. . . . He alone is sufficient for the heart, who made it. I do not say, of course, that nothing short of the Almighty Creator can awaken and answer to our love, reverence, and trust; man can do this for man. Man doubtless is an object to rouse his brother's love, and repays it in his measure. Nay, it is a great duty, one of the two chief duties of religion thus to be minded towards our neighbour. . . .

But there is another reason why God alone is the happiness of our souls, to which I wish rather to direct attention:—the contemplation of Him, and nothing but it, is able fully to open and relieve the mind,

1. *P.S.*, IV, p. 261 2. *P.S.*, V, pp. 324–6

to unlock, occupy, and fix our affections. We may indeed love things created with great intenseness, but such affection, when disjoined from the love of the Creator, is like a stream running in a narrow channel . . . it is not an expanding of the whole man. Created natures cannot open us, or elicit the ten thousand mental senses which belong to us, and through which we really live. None but the presence of our Maker can enter us; for to none besides can the whole heart in all its thoughts and feelings be unlocked and subjected. 'Behold' he says, 'I stand at the door and knock; if any man hear my voice and open the door, I will come in to him, and sup with him, and he with me.' . . . It is this feeling of simple and absolute confidence and communion, which soothes and satisfies those to whom it is vouchsafed.[1]

God has made us for Himself, and it is the great Christian privilege that He gives Himself to us. Newman returns again and again to the Divine Indwelling:

A true Christian, then, may almost be defined as one who has a ruling sense of God's presence within him. As none but justified persons have that privilege, so none but the justified have that practical perception of it. . . . In all circumstances, of joy or sorrow, hope or fear, let us aim at having Him in our inmost heart; let us have no secret apart from Him. Let us acknowledge Him as enthroned within us at the very springs of thought and affection. . . . This is the true life of saints. This is to have the Spirit witnessing with our spirits that we are sons of God. . . .[2]

Similarly in 'The Spritual Presence of Christ in The Church':

Christians looking back on years past, will feel, at least in a degree, that Christ has been with them, though they knew it not, only believed it at the time. They will even recollect the burning of their hearts. . . . They will experience a sort of heavenly fragrance and savour of immortality, when they least expect it, rising upon their minds, as if in token that God has been with them.[3]

In these passages we see Newman describing the experimental knowledge of God. For the most part in the *Parochial Sermons* and in *Lectures on Justification* he describes the New Testament teaching on the presence of God in the souls of true believers. Following the pattern of the New Testament, he has much to say about this objective Presence and privilege, and less to say about the experience to which it may lead. In fact, Newman's mystical

1. *P.S.*, V, pp. 316–8
2. *P.S.*, V, pp. 225–6, 236
3. *P.S.*, VI, p. 134

teaching is simply that of St John and St Paul, the revealed mysticism, expounded at Oxford with wonderful clarity; and like the mysticism of St John and St Paul, Newman's is wholly incarnational, wholly dependent on Christ. Here we have the purest doctrine of the New Testament, free from those extraneous influences which are to be found in so many of the Christian mystics.

We come, then, to Newman on our Lord. The last sermon in the sixth volume of *Parochial Sermons*, 'Peace in believing,' is perhaps the most perfect outline in English of the Revelation the Father has made through His Son and His Spirit.[1] Here is no arid speculation, but the richness of revealed truth, and we are enabled to *realise* the doctrine of the Incarnation. The sermon is too long to quote, as is the Sermon in the fourth volume on 'Watching' ('Do you know the feeling in matters of this life, of expecting a friend, expecting him to come and he delays'[2]) but here are some other sentences about Christ, the centre of the Christian life. A sermon on Christmas begins:

> Our Saviour's birth in the flesh is an earnest, and, as it were, beginning of our birth in the Spirit. It is a figure, promise, or pledge of our new birth, and it effects what is promises. . . . As He is the Son of God by nature, so are we sons of God by grace. . . .
>
> He, who is the everlasting Light, became the Light of men. . . . And when He came into the world, He was a pattern of sanctity in the circumstances of His life.[3]

This implies meditating on Christ, which 'is simply this, thinking habitually and constantly of Him and of His deeds and sufferings. It is to have Him before our minds . . . when we are at home and abroad, when we are working, or walking, or at rest, when we are alone, and again when we are in company'.[4]

In a famous sermon on the Passion Newman wrote:

> Now I bid you consider that that Face, so ruthlessly smitten, was the Face of God Himself; the Brows bloody with the thorns, the sacred Body exposed to view and lacerated with the scourge, the Hands nailed to the Cross, and, afterwards, the Side pierced with the spear; it was the Blood, and the sacred Flesh, and the Hands, and the Temples, and the Side, and the Feet of God Himself, which the frenzied multitude

1. *P.S.*, VI, pp. 362–71
2. *P.S.*, IV, p. 322
3. *P.S.*, V, pp. 86, 93
4. *P.S.*, VI, p. 41

then gazed upon. This is so fearful a thought, that when the mind first masters it, surely it will be difficult to think of anything else.[1]

James Anthony Froude heard these words in St Mary's and wrote long afterwards:

It was as if an electric stroke had gone through the church, as if every person present understood for the first time the meaning of what he had all his life been saying. I suppose it was an epoch in the mental history of more than one of my Oxford contemporaries.[2]

Then in the Sermon, 'The Cross of Christ the Measure of the World', Newman shows the Crucifixion of the Son of God as the key to the Christian interpretation of life. 'It is the death of the Eternal Word of God, made flesh, which is our lesson how to think and how to speak of this world.' It 'has put its due value upon every thing which we see, upon all fortunes, all advantages, all ranks, all dignities, all pleasures . . .' 'Go to the political world . . . to the world of intellect and science . . . look at misery, look at poverty and destitution, look at oppression and captivity; go where food is scanty and lodging unhealthy. . . . Would you know how to rate all these? gaze upon the Cross.'[3]

The Passion, too, is the origin of the pardon and regeneration of man. From it, Baptism derives its power, as do the other sacraments, and through them we reach Christ, even experience His presence.

A thick black veil is spread between this world and the next. . . . In the Gospel this veil is not removed; it remains, but every now and then marvellous disclosures are made to us of what is behind it. At times we seem to catch a glimpse of a Form which we shall hereafter see face to face. We approach, and in spite of the darkness, our hands, or our head, or our brow, or our lips become, as it were, sensible of the contact of something more than earthly. We know not where we are, but we have been bathing in water, and a voice tells us that it is blood. Or we have a mark signed upon our foreheads, and it spake of Calvary. Or we recollect a hand laid upon our heads, and surely it had the print of nails in it, and resembled His who with a touch gave sight to the blind and raised the dead. Or we have been eating and drinking; and it was not a dream surely, that One fed us from His wounded side, and renewed our nature by the heavenly meat He gave. Thus in many ways

1. *P.S.*, VI, p. 74
2. 'The Oxford Counter Reformation', in *Short Studies on Great Subjects*, London 1907, V, pp. 206–7
3. *P.S.*, VI, pp. 84–6

He who is to judge us, prepares us to be judged,—He, who is to glorify us, prepares us to be glorified, that He may not take us unawares.[1]

In this collection of 'liturgical homilies', after those on the Passion, come a whole series on 'rising with Christ':

It is then the duty and privilege of all disciples of our glorified Saviour, to be exalted and transfigured with Him; to live in heaven in their thoughts, motives, aims, desires, likings, prayers, praises, intercessions, even while they are in the flesh; to look like other men, to be busy like other men, to be passed over in the crowd of men or even to be scorned or oppressed, as other men may be, but the while to have a secret channel of communication with the Most High, a gift the world knows not of; to have their life *hid* with Christ in God.[2]

In the sermon, 'Waiting for Christ,' Newman sums up: 'No higher Priest could come,—no truer doctrine. The Light and Life of men had appeared, and had suffered, and had risen again; and nothing more was left to do . . . and therefore it was the last time', until Christ's second coming.[3]

Newman's full and balanced exposition did not stop, as was so often the case in his day and since, with the contemplation of Our Lord's Passion.

There is another ground for saying that Christ did not finish his gracious economy by His death; viz. because the Holy Spirit came in order to finish it. When He ascended, He did not leave us to ourselves; so far the work was not done. He sent His Spirit. . . . To Him are committed to apply to us all that Christ had done for us. As then His mission proves on the one hand that salvation is not from ourselves, so does it on the other that it must be wrought in us. For if all gifts of grace are with the Spirit, and the presence of the Spirit is within us, it follows that these gifts are to be manifested and wrought in us. If Christ is our sole hope, and Christ is given to us by the Spirit, and the Spirit be an inward presence, our sole hope is in an inward change. As a light placed in a room pours out its rays on all sides, so the presence of the Holy Ghost imbues us with life, strength, holiness, love, acceptableness, righteousness. . . . That divine influence, which has the fulness of Christ's grace to purify us, has also the power of Christ's blood to justify. . . . Christ Himself vouchsafes to repeat in each of us in figure and mystery all that He did and suffered in the flesh. He is formed in us, born in us, suffers in us, rises again in us, lives in

1. *P.S.*, V, pp. 10–11
2. *P.S.*, VI, p. 214
3. *P.S.*, VI, pp. 240–1

us . . . and this divine presence constitutes the title of each of us to heaven. . . .[1]

Again and again in the Sermons, Newman returns to the truth, 'that the Holy Ghost is come; but why has He come? to supply Christ's absence or to accomplish His presence? Surely to make Him present.'[2]

In *Lectures on Justification* Newman makes this even clearer, and depicts for us the Paschal Mystery, the Easter Faith of Christianity: 'Whatever is done in the Church since Christ's Ascension, is done by the Spirit.' This is implied by the text that Christ who died for our sins 'rose again for our justification' and 'it implies that justification is through that second Comforter whom that resurrection brought down from heaven'. Hence:

> Christ's work of mercy has two chief parts, as specified in the text; what He did for all men, what He does for each; what He did once for all, what He does for one by one continually; what He did externally to us, what He does within us; what He did on earth, what He does in heaven; what He did in His own Person, what He does by His Spirit; His death, and the water and blood after it; His meritorious sufferings, and the various gifts thereby purchased, of pardon, grace, reconciliation, renewal, holiness, spiritual communion; that is, His Atonement, and the application of His Atonement, or His Atonement and our justification; He atones by the offering of Himself on the Cross; and as certainly (which is the point before us) He justifies by the Mission of His Spirit. . . .
>
> He came once, He ascended back, He has come again. He came first in the flesh; He has come a second time in the Spirit. . . . As in God's counsels it was necessary for the Atonement that there should be a material, local, Sacrifice of the Son once for all: so for our individual justification, there must be a spiritual, ubiquitous communication of that Sacrifice continually. There was but one Atonement; there are ten thousand justifications . . .
>
> Further; it would appear as if His going to the Father was, in fact, the same thing as His coming to us spiritually. I mean there is some mysterious unknown connection between his departing in His own Person, and His returning in the Person of His Spirit. He said that unless He went, His Spirit would not come to us. . . . His rising, then, was the necessary condition of His applying to His elect the virtue of that Atonement which His dying wrought for all men. . . . Thus He died to purchase what He rose again to apply. 'He died for our sins;

1. *P.S.*, V, pp. 138–40 2. *P.S.*, VI, pp. 125–6

He rose again for our justification . . .' He atoned, I repeat, in His own Person. He justifies through His Spirit.

And here I have touched upon another part of the harmony of the Divine Dispensation, which may be profitably dwelt upon. He Himself was raised again and justified by the Spirit; and what was wrought in Him is repeated in us who are His brethren, and the complement and ratification of His work. What took place in Him as an Origin, is continued on in the succession of those who inherit His fulness, and is the cause of its continuance.[1]

Newman's conclusion of this lecture is that what he has said

. . . will serve to throw light upon a peculiarity of the Apostle's preaching, which has sometimes drawn attention. They insist on our Lord's Resurrection, as if it were the main doctrine of the Gospel; but why so, and not on His Divinity or the Atonement? Many good reasons may be given for this; as, for instance, that the Resurrection was the great miracle and evidence of the divinity of the religion. . . . But if, as we have seen, the Resurrection be the means by which the Atonement is applied to each of us, if it be our justification, if in it are conveyed all the gifts of grace and glory which Christ has purchased for us, if it be the commencement of His giving Himself to us for our spiritual sustenance . . . it is that very doctrine which is most immediate to us, in which Christ most closely approaches us, from which we gain life, and out of which issue our hopes and our duties. Christ is God from everlasting; He became man under Caesar Augustus; He was an Atonement for the world on the Cross; but He became a Saviour on His resurrection.[2]

From the New Testament doctrine that the Spirit is on earth because the Son is in heaven, it follows that at Pentecost the Holy Spirit was given not merely more abundantly than before, but, apart from the exceptions God may choose to make, for the first time. There is very little about the Holy Spirit as sanctifier in the Old Testament, and St John is entirely in line with St Paul when he says, 'as yet the Spirit was not given, because Jesus was not yet glorified'. This was the teaching of the Greek Fathers, to whom Newman was so devoted, and of Petavius. The Holy Spirit was given dynamically only in the Old Testament, substantially in the New. Newman points out that the indwelling was promised as the *distinguishing* grace of the Gospel.

St Paul declares both the prophecy and its fulfilment, when he says: 'Ye are the temple of the living God; as God hath said, I will dwell in

1. *Jfc.*, pp. 203–7 2. *Jfc.*, pp. 221–2

them, and walk in them; and I will be their God, and they shall be my people.'

The same acceptableness before God can come in different ways, and what 'at first sight seems a difficulty, that the attribute of righteousness, however conveyed to the Old Saints, should since Christ's coming be attendant on a divine gift, even His own sacred Presence,' is 'an argument in favour of the doctrine. For such a transformation of shadows into substances, and human acts into divine endowments, far from being anomalous, is the very rule of the New Covenant.'[1]

In the very year that Newman was delivering the *Lectures on Justification* Pusey was being attacked by the Evangelicals for holding that the grace of the Old Testament differed in kind from that of the New. They described this opinion as 'the very bathos of theology'. Newman came to his rescue with an open letter, and pointed out that as the Evangelicals overlooked the doctrine of a Divine Presence in the soul, there was no grace they ascribed to the Christian, which Pusey did not ascribe to Abraham. When Newman edited this letter in 1877 he added a note which shows that he still held 'that the Jews had not the gift of regeneration, and that they had not the indwelling of the Holy Ghost, both of these being the privilege of Christians'. He preached the same doctrine in the *Sermons*, e.g.: 'If the Jews had not received the promised Spirit, it is not wonderful that they did not show forth the special fruits of that Spirit which was promised. . . . Some graces they had because they had faith; all they had not, because they had not the Indwelling Spirit.'[2]

Similarly in *Lectures on Justification* Newman points out that Christ came 'to new-create,—to begin a new line, and construct a new kingdom on the earth'. 'Henceforth He is the one principle of life in all His servants, who are but His organs. The Jewish Church looked towards Him; the Christian speaks and acts from Him,' and has become His body.

Newman's conclusion is that:

. . . whatever might be the righteousness of the Jews, we certainly know what is ours; and it is what they could not have had. It is 'Christ', our propitiation, 'within us'. . . . It is a more simple theory, doubtless, to say that righteousness should be to the Christian what it

1. *Jfc.*, pp. 147 and 193
2. *V.M.*, II, pp. 166–7, *P.S.*, VI, p. 179

was to the Jew. . . . But those who believe that Christ has set up a new creation in unity, and that He Himself is the One principle in His Church, of all grace and truth, will not be surprised to find that He has superseded the righteousness, as He has abolished the victims, of the ancient time; and that as the grace of the Holy Eucharist is the Presence of Christ Crucified, so the justification of those who approach it is the Indwelling of Christ risen and glorified.[1]

Newman insists on our union with Christ the Incarnate Word, and His Presence in the soul which the Spirit secures. Earlier in the *Lectures* he wrote:

Let it be remarked that the Divine Presence vouchsafed to us, besides being that of the Holy Trinity, is specially said to be the presence of Christ; which would seem to imply that the 'Word made flesh', is in some mysterious manner bestowed upon us.[2]

This was not to be an accepted teaching among the Roman theologians until the second half of the twentieth century. Hence in the preface to the third edition of the *Lectures* in 1874, Newman felt it necessary to justify what he had written, and quoted from the *Theologia Mystica* of Schram, in favour of 'a Personal Presence of our Lord in the soul, apart from His Incarnate Presence which is vouchsafed in the Eucharist'. Recently, a Roman theologian, Hugo M. de Achaval, S.J., has written:

In his *Lectures on Justification*—his most theological work—Newman explains at length the ancient doctrine of the indwelling not only of the Holy Spirit but of the Word Incarnate too, which from the time of the Fathers had been over-shadowed by the scholastic controversies of the sixteenth century. Against Protestants and against a certain decadent Catholic theology, which had lost contact with its proper sources, Newman's theology about uncreated grace, which is for him the first and last scope of the Incarnation, is to be found today among the most modern and learned theologians, and . . . in the Encyclical Letter on the Mystical Body of Christ.[3]

About the Church as the Body of Christ, Newman has this to say:

We have lost Christ and we have found Him; we see Him not, yet we discern Him. We embrace His feet, yet He says, 'Touch me not'. How is this? it is thus: we have lost the sensible and conscious perception

1. *Jfc.*, pp. 194–6, 200–1 2. *Jfc.*, p. 148
3. *Newman's Apologia: A Classic Reconsidered*, edited by V. F. Blehl, S.J. and F. X. Connolly, New York 1964, p. 137

of Him; we do not look on Him, hear Him, converse with Him, follow Him from place to place; but we enjoy the spiritual, immaterial, inward, mental, real sight and possession of Him; a possession more real and more present than that which the Apostles had in the days of His flesh, *because* it is spiritual, *because* it is invisible. . . . Christ has come so close to us in the Christian Church (if I may so speak), that we cannot gaze on Him or discern Him. He enters into us, He claims and takes possession of His purchased inheritance; He does not present Himself to us, but He takes us to Him. He makes us His members.[1]

And this:

Christ formed His Apostles into a visible society; but when He came again in the person of His Spirit, He made them all in a real sense one, not in name only. For they were no longer arranged merely in the form of unity, as the limbs of the dead may be, but they were parts and organs of one unseen power; they really depended upon, and were offshoots of that which was One; their separate persons were taken into a mysterious union with things unseen, were grafted upon and assimilated to the spiritual body of Christ, which is one, even by the Holy Ghost, in whom Christ has come again to us. Thus Christ came, not to make us one but to die for us: the Spirit came to make us one in Him who had died and was alive, that is, to form the Church.

This then is the special glory of the Christian Church, that its members do not depend merely on what is visible, they are not mere stones of a building, piled one on another, and bound together from without, but they are one and all the births and manifestations of one and the same unseen spiritual principle or power, '*living* stones', internally connected, as branches from a tree, not as the parts of a heap. They are members of the Body of Christ. That divine and adorable Form, which the Apostles saw and handled, after ascending into heaven became a principle of life, a secret origin of existence to all who believe, though the gracious ministration of the Holy Ghost. . . . So that in a true sense it may be said, that from the day of Pentecost to this hour there has been in the Church but One Holy One, the King of kings, and Lord of lords Himself, Who is in all believers, and through whom they are what they are; their separate persons being but as separate developments, vessels, instruments, and works of Him who is invisible.[2]

Newman gave much attention to the Holy Eucharist, the means of union with Christ. Although he did not accept the doctrine of transubstantiation, he wrote as follows in the sermon on 'The Eucharistic Presence':

1. *P.S.*, VI, p. 121 2. *P.S.*, IV, pp. 169–70

Nothing can show more clearly how high the blessing is, than to observe that the Church's tendency has been, not to detract from its marvellousness, but to increase it. The Church has never thought little of the gift; so far from it, we know that one very large portion of Christendom holds more than we do. That belief, which goes beyond ours, shows how great the gift is really. I allude to the doctrine of what is called transubstantiation . . . [1]

Thus Newman put forward the great Christian privileges, but, with his horror of unreality in religion, he was emphatic and relentless in telling us the price to be paid, before Christ's love can take possession of us.

I must say plainly this, that fanciful though it may appear at first sight, the comforts of life are the main cause of our want of love of God; and, much as we may lament and struggle against it, till we learn to dispense with them in good measure, we shall not overcome it. Till we, in a certain sense, detach ourselves from our bodies, our minds will not be in a state to receive divine impressions, and to exert heavenly aspirations. A smooth and easy life, an uninterrupted enjoyment of the goods of Providence, full meals, soft raiment, well-furnished homes, the pleasures of sense, the feeling of security, the consciousness of wealth,—these and the like, if we are not careful, choke up all the avenues of the soul, through which the light and breath of heaven might come to us. . . . If we attempt to force our minds into a loving and devotional temper, without this preparation, it is too plain what will follow—the grossness and coarseness, the affectation, the effeminacy, the unreality, the presumption, the hollowness, (suffer me, my brethren, while I say plainly but seriously what I mean,) in a word, what Scripture calls the Hypocrisy, which we see around us.[2]

Newman insists:

When a man comes to God to be saved, then, I say, the essence of true conversion is a *surrender* of himself, an unreserved, unconditional surrender. . . . What then is it that we who profess religion lack? I repeat it, this: a willingness to *be* changed, a willingness to suffer (if I may use such a word), to suffer Almighty God to change us. We do not like to let go our old selves.[3]

Owing to Newman's insistence on self-denial in religion, on the gravity of sin, and on the costliness of union with God, he has been accused of rigorism and pessimism. This must be seen

1. *P.S.*, VI, p. 141
2. *P.S.*, V, pp. 337–8
3. *P.S.*, V, p. 241

in its setting. As Father Faber remarked in 1850: 'I am hardly a fair judge of *your* sternness, because in old times you were the *relief* to Pusey's oppressive Novatianism; Manning was between you and was much less lightsome than you. At the same time I suppose ladies taking to the parochial sermons is no proof they were not stern to a certain point, for there seems a kind of sternness in English earnestness, and spiritual things won't go down in England without it.'[1] Newman may be stern, but he shows how peace and joy are the keynotes of the Christian character:

Gloom is no Christian temper; that repentance is not real, which has not love in it; that self-chastisement is not acceptable, which is not sweetened by faith and cheerfulness. We must live in sunshine, even when in sorrow; we must live in God's presence, we must not shut ourselves up in our own hearts, even when we are reckoning up our past sins.[2]

. . . The Christian has a deep, silent, hidden peace, which the world sees not,—like some well in a retired and shady place, difficult of access. He is the greater part of his time by himself, and what he is in solitude, that is his real state. What he is when left to himself and to his God, that is his true life. He can bear himself; he can (as it were) joy in himself, for it is the grace of God within him, it is the presence of the Eternal Comforter in which he joys. He can bear, he finds it pleasant, to be with himself at all times,—'never less alone than when alone'. He can lay his head on his pillow at night, and own in God's sight, with overflowing heart, that he wants nothing,—that he 'is full and abounds',—that God has been all things to him, and that nothing is not his which God could give him. More thankfulness, more holiness, more of heaven he needs indeed, but the thought that he can have more is not a thought of trouble, but of joy. It does not interfere with his peace to know that he may grow nearer to God. . . . The Christian is cheerful, easy, kind, gentle, courteous, candid, unassuming; has no pretence, no affectation, no ambition, no singularity; because he has neither hope nor fear about this world. He is serious, sober, discreet, grave, moderate, mild, with so little that is unusual or striking in his bearing, that he may easily be taken at first sight for an ordinary man. There are persons who think religion consists in ecstasies, or in set speeches;—he is not of those.[3]

And finally:

We are Christ's, not by faith merely, or by works merely, but by love. . . . We are saved . . . by that heavenly flame within us, which, while it

1. *L. and D.*, XIII, p. 427
2. *P.S.*, V, p. 271
3. *P.S.*, V, pp. 69–71

consumes what is seen, aspires to what is unseen. Love is the gentle, tranquil, satisfied acquiescence and adherence of the soul in the contemplation of God; not only a preference of God before all things, but a delight in Him because He is God, and because His commandments are good . . .[1]

Newman was a Christian humanist; he made his own the joyful optimism which pervades the teaching of St Ambrose, St Athanasius and the Greek Fathers. His spiritual doctrine was intended for and is adapted to those in the world, ordinary laymen. A famous sermon, first preached at the end of 1836, 'Doing glory to God in Pursuit of the World,' begins:

When persons are convinced that life is short . . . when they feel that the next life is all in all, and that eternity is the only subject that really can claim or can fill their thoughts, then they are apt to undervalue this life altogether, and to forget its real importance. They are apt to wish to spend the time of their sojourning here in a positive separation from active and social duties: yet it should be recollected that the employments of this world, though not themselves heavenly, are, after all the way to heaven . . . but it is difficult to realize this. It is difficult to realize both truths at once, and to connect both truths together; steadily to contemplate the life to come, yet to act in this. . . .

In various ways does the thought of the next world lead men to neglect their duty in this; and whenever it does so we may be sure that there is something wrong and unchristian, not in their thinking of the next world, but in their manner of thinking of it.

Newman suggests various remedies, among them being this:

The Christian will feel that the true contemplation of his Saviour lies *in* his worldly business; that as Christ is seen in the poor, and in the persecuted, and in children, so is He seen in the employments He puts upon His chosen, whatever they be; that in attending to his own calling he will meet Christ; that if he neglect it, he will not on that account enjoy His presence at all the more, but that while performing it, he will see Christ revealed to his soul amid the ordinary actions of the day, as by a sort of sacrament.[2]

Newman's high idea of God's majesty gives his sermons their seriousness and reverence. He is conscious, too, and helps his readers to face the terrible mysteries:

No thought of course is more overpowering than that every one who lives or has lived is destined for endless bliss or torment. It is far too vast to realize.

1. *P.S.*, IV, pp. 317–18 2. *P.S.*, VIII, pp. 154, 165

And he asks:

How shall we persuade ourselves of the great truth that, in spite of outward appearances, human society as we find it, is but a part of an invisible world, and is really divided into two companies, the sons of God, and the children of the wicked one . . .[1]

In the Sermon already mentioned, 'Peace in Believing,' we are told to trust, in the midst of these sobering truths:

All God's providences, all God's dealings with us, all His judgments, mercies, warnings, deliverances, tend to peace and repose as their ultimate issue. All our troubles and pleasures here, all our anxieties, fears, doubts, difficulties, hopes, encouragements, afflictions, losses, attainments, tend this one way. . . . After our soul's anxious travail; after the birth of the Spirit; after trial and temptation; after sorrow and pain; after daily dyings to the world; after daily risings into holiness; at length comes that 'rest which remaineth unto the people of God'.

Matthew Arnold long afterwards quoted the sentences that immediately follow those above.

Forty years ago Newman was in the very prime of life; he was close at hand to us at Oxford; he was preaching in St Mary's pulpit every Sunday; he seemed about to transform and to renew what was for us the most national and natural institution in the world, the Church of England. . . . I seem to hear him still saying:

'After the fever of life; after wearinesses and sicknesses; fightings and despondings, languor and fretfulness; struggling and failing, struggling and succeeding; after all the changes and chances of this troubled unhealthy state, at length comes death, at length the white throne of God, at length the Beatific Vision.[2]

1. *P.S.*, IV, pp. 87, 91

2. *P.S.*, VI, pp. 369–70: *Discourses in America*, London 1885, pp. 139–40. Arnold seems not actually to have heard this sermon. It was last delivered on 6 June 1841, and he did not come up to Oxford until October 1841.

CHAPTER 5

The Last Years as a Leader: Retirement and Rome (1838-45)

SINCE 'example is always more efficacious than precept', Newman published in 1838, in association with Keble, the *Remains of Richard Hurrell Froude*, extracts from his private journal and letters. These revealed not only Froude's rejection of the Reformers and his hold on Catholic truths, but the life of prayer, fasting and self-discipline that he had been leading for years. This picture of a Tractarian 'saint' caused a furore in Protestant England. In the preface Newman wrote to the first volume of the *Remains* he defended Froude against the charge of Romanism, defined as 'an overweening value for outward religion, for Sacraments, Church polity, public worship,—such a respect for these, as renders a man comparatively inattentive (so it is surmised) to the inward and spiritual part of religion'. Newman thought Froude's papers showed that Catholic views were 'perfectly consistent, nay, inseparably bound up, with the most elevated notions of inward sanctification, of a renewed heart and life'.[1] In spite of the precautions Newman and Keble took, English Protestantism was scandalised, and the publication of the *Remains* stiffened the opposition to the Tractarians. There were, nevertheless, plenty of people at Oxford and elsewhere ready to respond to the Gospel ideal of holiness that was being put before them in Newman's preaching and printed sermons. William Lockhart, who came up to Oxford in 1838, contrasts the extraordinary purity in those days among the young women of the upper and middle classes, with that of their brothers, who were sent away from home to public school. It was these young men who then went up to Oxford, and on them 'Newman's sermons came down like a new revelation. He had the wondrous, the supernatural power of raising the mind to God, and of rooting deeply in us a personal

1. *Remains of Richard Hurrell Froude*, London 1838, I, pp. x and xvi

conviction of God, and a sense of His Presence. He compelled us to an intuitive perception of moral obligation—of that Natural Law of right, which is written in the mind by the word and wisdom of God'.[1] John Duke Coleridge went up to Oxford in 1839 and gave his testimony in the House of Commons, in 1867, when p oposing the second reading of a bill to enable Nonconformists to become Fellows of Oxford Colleges. To those who opposed him with the argument that this would undermine the religious teaching given by the Established Church, he replied that for many years 'the prevailing temper of the Governors of Oxford has been steadily set against religious earnestness', and he cited the case of Newman, who met with cold aversion and steady discouragement on the part of the authorities.

There was a man in my time of admirable genius, of rare eloquence, of saintly life, of singular humility and self-denial, who taught us not any peculiar theological dogma, but simple religious truth; whose example kept a lofty standard before our eyes; who led us by his life and by his teaching to all things 'lovely and of good report'; to whom many in Church and State owe it that their sense of responsibility was awakened, and that they are now, in their degree, doing in some poor and imperfect way, their duty both to God and man.[2]

A lady, typical of many, Miss Parker, an Eton 'dame', wrote: 'I have listened to you with the ear often . . . by the written word you have been my teacher for years'.[3]

One striking testimony to the effect of Newman's preaching at Oxford is the sermon he felt it necessary to preach there on 30 October 1842, on the 'Dangers of the Penitent'. He warned repentant sinners not to be impatient. They wanted to undertake some humble task or state of life, without waiting to see how God would use them. They wanted to overburden themselves with prayer and penance, or to make rash vows of continence. Newman insisted that they must count the cost, begin with small humiliations, and take advice. The dangers of the penitent were not in the direction of outward exhibitions of intemperate zeal, but towards a hidden life of sacrifice and self-denial. That was the

1. William Lockhart, *Cardinal Newman*, London 1891, pp. 25–6
2. E. H. Coleridge, *Life and Correspondence of Lord Coleridge*, London 1908, II, p. 49, Hansard's *Parliamentary Debates*, CLXXXV, p. 1423
3. *L. and D.*, XI, p. 351

'danger' to which Newman's preaching gave rise. He realised the change, as a sermon earlier in the year, on 1 May, shows:

There is at this moment a growing feeling of the beauty of religion, a growing reverence for, and insight into the privileges of the Gospel. Persons begin to understand far more than they did, that Christianity is not a mere law, a Jewish yoke, but a new law, a service of freedom, a rule of spirit and truth, which wins us as well as commands, and influences us while it threatens. Hitherto, it has seemed as if all sense of the privileges and pleasures of religion were possessed by those who had but erroneous views of doctrine . . . but all this is gone by. A more primitive, Catholic, devout, ardent spirit, is abroad among the holders of orthodox truth. The piercing, and thrilling, and kindling, and enrapturing glories of the Kingdom of Christ, are felt in their degree by many. Men are beginning to understand that influence, which in the beginning made the philosopher leave his school, and the soldier beat his spear into a pruning-hook.[1]

Newman's chief concern was the revival of Revealed Religion, but this broadened rather than limited his interests. James Anthony Froude wrote of him at this period, when he himself was at Oxford:

Newman's mind was world-wide. He was interested in everything which was going on in science, in politics, in literature. Nothing was too large for him, nothing too trivial, if it threw light upon the central question, what man really was, and what his destiny. . . . He could admire enthusiastically any greatness of action and character, however remote the sphere of it from his own.[2]

Although, long before he retired to Littlemore in 1842, Newman was leading a life of considerable austerity, this did not cut him off from others. His friends were as numerous and devoted as ever, acquaintances found him fascinating. At the beginning of 1837 he began weekly soireés in his rooms for undergraduates, and these continued uninterrupted for the next four years. Miss Mitford has preserved the account of a plodding undergraduate she knew, invited by Newman regularly to breakfast. He was asked what they discussed. 'Everything,—the classics, history, mathematics, general literature. . . . In short he talks to me of every sort of subject except what is called Tractarianism, and that he has never

1. *Sermons on Subjects of the Day*, abbreviated as *S.D.*, pp. 41–51 and 114–15
2. 'The Oxford Counter-Reformation', in *Short Studies on Great Subjects*, London 1907, V, p. 201

mentioned.'[1] Not only were there the endless breakfast and dinner parties at Oxford, but when Newman visited London, it was the same. He was there in July 1840, dining with different friends each night, and when going through his diary in 1874, he wrote at this point: 'How all this impresses on me, Lusisti satis, edisti satis, atque, bibisti, Tempus abire tibi est!'

For example's sake, too, it was important to bring before men's minds the Christian life as it was lived in the early centuries, Revealed Religion in practice. In 1840 he published *The Church of the Fathers*, essays written earlier, in which he tried to bring out in biographical sketches the atmosphere, the sentiments and customs of the Early Church. He was one of the chief supporters of the Tractarian *Library of the Fathers*, translations of patristic writings, of which the first volume, Pusey's *Confessions of St Augustine*, appeared in 1838. Newman translated three volumes of the works of St Athanasius for the series. He also published a translation of Fleury's *Church History*, prefacing it with an essay on ecclesiastical miracles. The Church of England must become more like the Church of the Fathers. From 1838 to 1841 he edited the monthly *British Critic* and made it the very effective organ of the Tractarian movement.

He also continued to examine the intellectual basis of the Christian faith, the relations between faith and reason, which had preoccupied him from the time of his first conversion. *Sermons preached before the University of Oxford* appeared in 1843, and Newman then described it as 'the least theological book I have published'. The earlier sermons in this volume, those up to the end of 1832, have already been mentioned. The remainder, the last six, preached between 1839 and 1843, provide Newman's most vivid treatment of the subject of faith and reason. When re-reading them four years after their publication, he wrote in a letter:

I must say I think they are as a whole, the best things I have written, and I cannot believe they are not Catholic and will not be useful. Indeed there are times (I mean after reading them and the like) that feelings come upon me, which do not often else,—but then vividly—I mean the feeling that I have not been done justice to.[2]

1. *The Letters and Correspondence of John Henry Newman during his Life in the English Church*, edited by Anne Mozley, II, p. 225, note
2. *L. and D.*, XII, p. 32

Newman's fullest teaching is to be found in *A Grammar of Assent*, and will be considered in connection with that work, but what he has to say in the *Oxford Sermons* is fresher and not restrained by fears of being misunderstood by scholastic philosophers. He insists, against the apologists of the 'evidential' school, that, in fact, Christians accept and believe the truths of revelation for reasons distinct from the evidence usually produced in favour of them. Those who have given themselves to religion by faith, 'and stake their happiness upon it, have done so, not on an examination of the evidence, but from a spontaneous movement of the heart towards it'. So faith is 'the reasoning of a divinely enlightened mind', an act of the whole man, and not merely of the reasoning powers. It is a 'simple lifting of the mind to the Unseen God, without conscious reasoning or formal argument'. 'Those who believe in Christ, believe because they know Him to be the Good Shepherd; and they know Him by His voice; and they know His voice because they are His sheep. . . . The divinely enlightened mind sees in Christ the very Object whom it desires to love and worship.'[1] Faith, then, is essentially a grace, a gift, higher than reason. It is not based on evidence, which only comes in later to protect and vindicate it. 'A judge does not make men honest, but acquits and vindicates them: in like manner, Reason need not be the origin of Faith, as Faith exists in the very persons believing, though it does test and verify it.' Further, 'if children, if the poor, if the busy, can have true Faith, yet cannot weigh evidence, evidence is not the simple foundation on which Faith is built'.[2] Such people have not time to make minute investigations.

Faith, though a gift, is a free act. Men can choose whether they will believe or not. A man is responsible for his Faith. What, then, prevents Faith from being mere credulity or fanaticism? Newman replies first of all 'a right state of heart'. Right Faith is the Faith of a mind whose disposition, whose conscience is right.

> Does a child trust his parents because he has proved to himself they are such, and that they are able and desirous to do him good or from the instinct of affection?[3]

The moral sense enables men to judge rightly in matters of religious duty, just as experience can sharpen their powers in other spheres.

1. *U.S.*, pp. 225, 208, 253, 236
2. *U.S.*, pp. 183, 231
3. *U.S.*, pp. 235–6

Thus the shepherd can foretell the weather, and the general interpret information, apparently without reasoning.

> Consider the preternatural sagacity with which a great general knows what his friends and his enemies are about, and what will be the final result, and where, of their combined movements, and then say whether, if he were required to argue the matter in word or on paper, all his most brilliant conjectures might not be refuted, and all his producible reasons exposed as illogical.[1]

Faith, then is the acceptance of truths as a duty, under a sense of personal responsibility. This acceptance is mainly swayed by antecedent considerations, especially that of the likelihood of a Revelation. Thus Faith is in accordance with reason to this extent that, 'taken together with the antecedent probability that Providence will reveal Himself to mankind, such evidence of the fact, as is otherwise deficient, may be enough for conviction, even in the judgment of reason'. Then, too, men may and do have implicit reasons for their Faith, which they are incapable of developing. 'All men reason, but not all men can give a reason.' Newman insists on appealing to the psychological facts: 'It is no proof that persons are not possessed, because they are not conscious of an idea.'[2] Even in the case of those who are able to analyse and state the grounds of their beliefs, so often the ostensible reasons fail to do justice to those which are implicit.

> It is hardly too much to say, that almost all reasons formally adduced in moral inquiries, are rather specimens and symbols of the real grounds, than those grounds themselves. They do but approximate to a representation of the general character of the proof which the writer wishes to convey to another's mind. They cannot, like mathematical proof, be passively followed with an attention confined to what is stated, and with admission of nothing but what is urged. Rather, they are hints towards, and samples of, the true reasoning.[3]

As long as he remained in Oxford, Newman held rationalism at bay, and Pusey deplored his departure because, 'Newman, while he was with us, was its most powerful and successful antagonist'. Newman naturally opposed also Jeremy Bentham's utilitarianism, and the views of his disciple, Lord Brougham, who treated 'useful knowledge' as a substitute for religion. Sir Robert Peel, Leader of the Conservative Party, and an orthodox Churchman,

1. *U.S.*, pp. 217–18
2. *U.S.*, pp. 195, 259, 321
3. *U.S.*, p. 275

unthinkingly aired their views and somewhat disparaged Christian teaching in a speech at the opening of a reading-room in Tamworth, on 19 January 1841. John Walter III of *The Times* had just left Oxford, where he had come under Newman's spell. He now persuaded his father to get Newman to reply to Peel in *The Times*. The result was the seven sparkling *Letters of Catholicus*, the last of which appeared on 27 February 1841, the same day as *Tract 90*. Newman had often resisted the view that the acquisition of knowledge was the same thing as education, and that education could make men not merely wiser, but better. He insists: 'To know is one thing, to do is another; the two things are altogether distinct.' Sir Robert Peel 'makes no pretence of subduing the giant nature, in which we were born', and gives countenance to 'the theory that diversion is the instrument of improvement, and excitement the condition of right action'. And Newman makes the comparison: 'When a child cries, the nurserymaid dances it about, or points to the pretty black horses out of window, or shows how ashamed poll-parrot or poor puss must be of its tantarums.' This diversion of useful knowledge 'is the new art of living, offered to the labouring classes, we will say, for instance, in a severe winter, snow on the ground, glass falling, bread rising, coal at 20d. the cwt, and no work'.[1] All that was in the second letter. In the third we find: 'Glory, science, knowledge, and whatever other fine names we use, never healed a wounded heart, nor changed a sinful one.' 'You do not get rid of vice by human expedients; you can but use them according to circumstances, and in their place, as making the best of a bad matter. You must go to a higher source for renovation of the heart and will. You do but play a sort of "hunt the slipper" with the fault of our nature, till you go to Christianity.'[2] The letters must be read to appreciate their wit. Newman insisted that he treated science with respect and gratitude. 'I call it by their own name, "useful and entertaining knowledge" . . . and, as thinking Christianity something more than useful and entertaining, I want faith to come first, and utility and amusement to follow.' But Newman had no illusions.

People say to me, that it is but a dream to suppose that Christianity should regain the organic power in human society which it once

1. 'The Tamworth Reading Room', *Discussions and Arguments*, pp. 262, 264, 266, 268
2. *Op. cit.*, pp. 270, 273

possessed. I cannot help that. I never said it could. I am not a politician; I am proposing no measures, but exposing a fallacy and resisting a pretence.[1]

To the end of his days Newman opposed the tendency 'towards assigning political or civil motives for social and personal duties, and thereby withdrawing matters of conduct from the jurisdiction of religion'.[2] In his sermons he reminded men of their social duties and responsibilities and denounced unprincipled money-making, but as he wrote to a friend in 1883: 'It has never been my line to take up political or social questions, unless they came close to me as matters of personal duty.' His was always the personal, the sympathetic approach, and what appalled him in the work-houses and prisons was the heartlessness. He devoted much time to visiting and caring for the poor in St Clements, at Littlemore, and later in Birmingham. Charity begins at home, and, as has been seen, in early days he supported his own family. Later his charities were munificent, but the direct curing of the social ills of nineteenth-century England did not lie in his sphere of activity. In spite of the dominant opinion of the political economists that the attempt to remedy social ills was worse than the disease, the Tractarians soon showed their interest in improving the position of 'Christ's poor'. But *non omnia possumus omnes*. Newman was preoccupied with the fundamental spiritual problems, the right solution of which has more to do even with immediate human happiness than more tangible social reforms. The decline in religious belief was a social problem of the first order, indeed the deepest of all social problems. Since Newman's day men have learned what cruelty and tyranny can follow when the sacred character of the human person and the absolute value of the human soul are forgotten or denied. Newman had grim fore-bodings of what he called the special peril of our time, the spread of the plague of infidelity. 'I think,' he says in a prophetic sermon in 1873, 'the trials which lie before us are such as would appal and make dizzy even such courageous hearts as St Athanasius and St Gregory, and they would confess that, dark as the prospect of their own day was to them severally, ours has a darkness

1. *Op. cit.*, pp. 280–1, 292
2. Letter to Canon Longman quoted in Terence Kenny, *The Political Thought of John Henry Newman*, London 1957, p. 172

different in kind from any that has been before it . . . Christianity has never yet had experience of a world simply irreligious'.[1]

Newman fully grasped, well before the start of the Oxford Movement, that in coming forward as the champion of Revealed Religion his real battle was with 'liberalism', that is, 'the anti-dogmatic principle', the subjecting of the truths of Revelation to human judgment.[2] So far the battle had on the whole gone well. It was true that the publication of Froude's *Remains* in 1838 had shocked many, and made the Protestants more vociferous than ever in their charge that the Tractarians were opening the Church of England to popery. But 'Catholic' views were spreading all the time, and with them a firmer grasp on revealed doctrine. The accusation of popery had often been made in the past against High Church Anglicans, and Newman felt that a chasm separated the English Church from that of Rome with her many corruptions. His balanced exposition of the Christian Faith, of which specimens have been given in the previous chapter, won support by its own inherent attractiveness. Perhaps then the *Via Media* would no longer be a 'paper religion', 'a mere modification either of Romanism or of popular Protestantism'. Perhaps Newman's own challenge, in his preface to *Lectures on the Prophetical Office*, would be answered: 'there certainly is a call upon us to exhibit our principles in action; and until we can produce diocese, or place of education, or populous town, or colonial department, or the like, administered on our distinctive principles . . . doubtless we have not as much to urge on our behalf as we might have'.[3] Before this could happen Newman discovered, as he thought, that the *Via Media* had existed in the distant past, there had been a time when it was not a 'paper religion'.

During the long vacation of 1839 he was studying the history of the Church in the fifth century. In 451, the Council of Chalcedon, urged on by Pope Leo the Great, had condemned Eutyches, who maintained that there was only one nature in Christ. He and his party were the extreme Monophysites, the Eutychians, but a moderate Monophysite party became very powerful in the Eastern Church. It claimed to reject Eutyches without fully accepting the decisions of the Council of Chalcedon. This party

1. *Catholic Sermons of Cardinal Newman*, edited at the Birmingham Oratory, London 1957, pp. 121, 123
2. *Apo.*, p. 48
3. *V.M.*, I, pp. 16–18

constituted a *Via Media* Church, 'Rome was where she now is; and the Protestants were the Eutychians'.[1] For those who accepted the Council of Chalcedon it was difficult to explain how the Eutychians and then the moderate Monophysites were heretics, unless Protestants and Anglicans were so as well; it was difficult to condemn the sixteenth-century popes and the Council of Trent without also condemning those of the fifth century and the Council of Chalcedon. This disturbing analogy was followed by another. In September 1839 Newman read an article in the *Dublin Review* by Nicholas Wiseman, still Rector of the English College at Rome, on the 'Anglican Claim to Apostolical Succession'. Newman did not feel the force of the parallel Wiseman drew between schismatic Donatists in North Africa in the time of St Augustine, and the Anglicans, but he was struck by St Augustine's way of deciding the controversy, his appeal to the general consent of Christians. 'Securus judicat orbis terrarum', the judgment of the whole world cannot be mistaken. This was a simpler way of deciding ecclesiastical questions than the appeal to the early centuries. That 'in which the whole Church at length rests and acquiesces, is an infallible prescription and a final sentence against such portions of it as protest and secede'. Newman has described graphically in the *Apologia* the effect upon him of this double shock.

He who has seen a ghost cannot be as if he has never seen it. The heavens had opened and closed again. The thought for the moment had been, 'The Church of Rome will be found right after all'; and then it had vanished. My old convictions remained as before.[2]

Newman's insular view of Christianity had received a blow, and he wrote immediately for the *British Critic* an answer to Wiseman, 'The Catholicity of the Anglican Church'. Newman urged that the principle 'securus judicat orbis terrarum' was not a rigorous regulation that allowed no exception. He admitted that it seemed easier to show that the Anglican Church lacked Catholicity than that the Roman had added to the Faith.

It is very obvious to the whole world that the English Church is separated from the rest of Christendom; it is not evident, except to a very few, that the faith of Rome is an addition to the primitive.

1. *Apo.*, pp. 114–15 2. *Apo.*, pp. 116–18

The Roman claim was that its additions were developments of revelation. The Anglican rejection of this raised a great problem.

It is still a difficulty how the great body of Christians should have gone wrong, even granting our assumption that they have; it is no difficulty that the great body should have added to the faith, when we grant their assumption that they have the power.

Newman resisted this assumption manfully. Developments were not admissible. 'Does the Church,' he asked, 'know more now than the Apostles knew?'[1] He then argued that, 'In spite of our being separated from Greece and Rome, shut up in ourselves and our dependencies, and looked coldly at and forgotten by the rest of Christendom, there is sufficient ground for still believing that the English Church is at this time the Catholic Church in England'.[2] For the moment, for two years in fact, until the summer of 1841, all was well. During that summer, as Newman began translating the treatises of St Athanasius against Arius, suddenly the history of the Arians and the semi-Arians appeared in a new light. The phenomenon of the Monophysites was repeated. The Arians were like the Protestants, the semi-Arians followed a *Via Media* like the Anglicans, and again 'Rome now was what it was then'. 'The ghost had come a second time.'[3]

Meanwhile others had read Wiseman's 1839 article, and the ghost was beginning to appear to them also. In reviving the forgotten doctrines about the 'Catholic' Church as a body essentially autonomous and deriving its authority ultimately from the Apostles, the Tractarians intended to provide a basis for resisting the encroachments of the State. But this assertion of independence at once drew attention to the problem of the isolated position of the Church of England in the 'Church Catholic'. Further, the moral and ascetical ideals to which Newman was winning so many people were the cause of their looking towards that Church which seemed specially to provide for and encourage those who were seeking after holiness. Newman realised this, and it led him, as he explained in the *Apologia*, to preach 'earnestly against the danger of being swayed in religious inquiry by our sympathy rather than by our reason'.[4] What perhaps inclined men even more to look Romewards was a growing conviction, as they pursued their studies, that there was

1. *Essays Critical and Historical*, II, pp. 11–12
2. *Op. cit.*, p. 47
3. *Apo.*, p. 139
4. *Apo.*, p. 165

so much Protestantism embedded in the Church of England as to invalidate its claim to be a branch of the Catholic Church. Its doctrine, as set forth in the official formulary, the Thirty-nine Articles, appeared to be clearly and deliberately Protestant. It was to meet this difficulty and to keep within the Anglican Church, by showing it to be genuinely Catholic, the many who were yearning after Rome, that Newman wrote *Tract 90*. This, the last and most famous of the *Tracts for the Times*, was published on 27 February 1841. It aimed at showing that the Thirty-nine Articles, although admittedly their animus was un-Catholic and they were not intended to inculcate Catholic doctrine, did not in their literal sense contradict it, and could be accepted by those who believed the Catholic truths as expounded by the Tractarians. *Tract 90* gave two main arguments for this Catholic interpretation: the first was historical, that, in fact, the Thirty-nine Articles were drawn up early in the reign of Elizabeth I in such a way as to induce moderate Roman Catholics to subscribe to them; and the second logical, that since the Anglican Church was a branch of the Catholic, its formularies must admit of being interpreted in accordance with what the Church Catholic had held from primitive times. In fact the Anglican Convocation which approved the Thirty-nine Articles had spoken with respect of 'the Catholic Fathers and Ancient Bishops'. Keble read *Tract 90* before it was published, and he and Pusey always upheld it. Newman, to the end of his life, professed himself satisfied with the substance of its argument, except that in his later years he expressed dissatisfaction with his reasoning about Article 31 on 'the sacrifice of masses'.[1]

On the other hand, Newman knew perfectly well that the Thirty-nine Articles bound him to oppose some of the Roman doctrines, and he approved of this. He considered that the practical Roman teaching on Purgatory, Indulgences, the honours paid to images and relics, the invocation of saints, and the mass, was not reconcilable with primitive Catholic doctrine. He thought that just as Rome had allowed exaggeration in those directions, Anglicanism had given in to exaggerations of Protestantism. In fact, there was an underlying irenical purpose in *Tract 90*. Newman admitted that there were 'practical and popular errors' on both sides, and tried to see how far the Thirty-nine Articles could be reconciled with the decrees of the Council of Trent,

1. *V.M.*, II, pp. 351–6

assuming the Roman Church to be ready to reform her practical teaching. The branch theory required that Rome and England should both belong to the one Catholic Church, and it was important to show that the differences between them were not radical. The Catholicity of the Church of England must be brought out, and that of the churches in communion with Rome admitted. It would have been too great a *reductio ad absurdum* of the branch theory to deny that Rome was substantially Catholic. Wiseman at once saw *Tract 90* as a possible basis of reunion between Anglicanism and Rome, while Dr Russell wrote from Maynooth to Newman that he looked forward, not to individual movements from the Church of England, 'but to see that church itself . . . bring itself into communion with ours'.

The immediate reaction, however, in Protestant England to *Tract 90* was far from being irenical. At Oxford the Board of Heads of Houses condemned Newman as a dishonest man, who in his *Tract* suggested that subscription to the Thirty-nine Articles might be reconciled with 'Roman Catholic error'. The Bishop of Oxford objected to the *Tract*, but eventually an understanding was reached with him that the bishops generally would not insist on its withdrawal nor condemn it, provided no further Tracts were issued. However, Newman found himself the object of considerable obloquy on the part of the Liberals at Oxford and the Evangelical party in general. His interpretation of *Tract 90*, although justified historically, came as a severe shock because the Articles had long been regarded as a bulwark of Protestantism. The understanding with the Bishop of Oxford proved ineffective, and in the course of the next three years the bishops took occasion in their Charges to condemn *Tract 90*. As Newman wrote in his *Letter to Pusey* in 1865:

> I considered my interpretation of the Articles, as I gave it in that Tract, would stand, provided the parties imposing them allowed it; otherwise, I thought it could not stand; and when in the event the Bishops and public opinion did not allow it, I gave up my Living.[1]

This he did not do until September 1843. He did nothing hastily, but it soon became clear that his position as leader of the great movement in the Church of England was untenable. A further blow to him, in the autumn of 1841, was the setting up in conjunction with the Protestants of Prussia of an Anglican bishopric

1. *Diff.*, II, p. 13

in Jerusalem. Just when Newman was being denounced for moving closer to Rome, the Anglican Church was moving away, fraternising with Protestants, and establishing a see in Eastern territory, in direct contradiction of the 'branch' theory of the Church. The decisive Anglican rejection of Catholic views now came to reinforce the doubts which his study of antiquity had first aroused.

Already in 1840 he had kept Lent out at Littlemore, every day fasting and abstaining severely, on Wednesdays and Fridays eating nothing until six in the evening, and reading no newspapers. At the end of 1841 he decided to retire there. Since subscription to the Thirty-nine Articles was required of all those who held office in the Church of England, and his interpretation of them had been rejected, he intended gradually to fall back into lay communion. He could not give up his responsibility for all those he had brought into the Movement, and he hoped it might be possible at a later period to restore the Catholic position in the Anglican Church. To join the Roman Church was out of the question, since Newman still considered she allowed honours to be paid to the Blessed Virgin and the saints, which were incompatible with the worship due to God alone. In retirement at Littlemore, he would avoid being the leader of a party opposed to the bishops of the Church, and in an atmosphere of prayer and penance he could think out the problems that faced him. Near the church he had built at Littlemore he took over a row of stables converted into rooms and made one into an oratory. A larger room held his great patristic library, which was moved there in February 1842. At the end of October 1842, he went up to Littlemore for good, and for most of the next three years had visitors or disciples sharing his life for longer or shorter periods, and to a greater or less extent. The system there was free and informal, but it was to prove a kind of starting-point of the regular religious life within the Anglican Church.

In February 1843 Newman preached a sermon on 'The Apostolical Christian', in which he argued that the true Bible Christians, the true 'Evangelicals' were those who joyfully left all things for Christ. The sermon was published at the end of the year, XIX, in *Sermons on Subjects of the Day*. This collection, as fine as any of the *Parochial Sermons*, was not, like them, purely ethical and doctrinal, for it often dealt with the immediate religious issues of the day. Also, as Newman explained in the preface, he sometimes added to the sermons as preached, expressions of more 'private or personal opinion' than was suitable for a parochial congregation. Four of these sermons, XXI–XXIV, preached on 28 November and 5, 12 and 19 December 1841, were, as Newman said in the *Apologia*, an attempt to meet the situation caused by the lesson of the history of Arianism, by the bishops' rejection of *Tract 90* and by the creation of the Jerusalem Bishopric. The Church of England seemed not only to him but to many of his followers to be proved undeniably Protestant, and to lack the external notes of the Church. He fell back in these four sermons on the theory that the Anglican Church was like the Ten Tribes, clearly separated from God's People, and yet somehow God's People still and with Prophets sent to it. The signs of religious experience, of a divine presence and life in the Anglican Church were sufficient to prove that she was not entirely outside the Catholic Church. 'The *Via Media* then disappeared for ever, and a Theory made expressly for the occasion, took its place.' Newman goes on to explain in the *Apologia* that his more moderate friends 'were naturally surprised and offended at a line of argument, novel, and, as it appeared to them, wanton, which threw the whole controversy into confusion, stultified my former principles, and substituted, as they would consider, a sort of methodistic self-contemplation, especially abhorrent both to my nature and to my past professions, for the plain and honest tokens, as they were commonly received, of a divine mission in the Anglican Church'.[1] The appeal to religious experience was a last despairing effort to hold up and prevent the secession of those who doubted.

Newman wrote *Tract 90* in order to prevent Anglicans from going over to Rome, and it was not until it had been decisively rejected that the conversions began. He himself, as his letters show, resisted the suggestions and premonitions that kept rising in his mind that the Roman claims might be well-founded. He did not give a *voluntary* assent to these thoughts, and tried to treat them as temptations. Not until the summer of 1843 did he fully recognise how things were going with him. On 4 May of that year he wrote to Keble of 'something which has at last been forced upon my full consciousness', confessing that 'as far as I can realise

1. *Apo.*, pp. 152–7

my own convictions, I consider the Roman Catholic Communion the Church of the Apostles, and that what grace is among us (which, through God's mercy, is not little) is extraordinary, and from the overflowings of His Dispensation'. Newman added: 'I am very far *more* sure that England is in schism, than that the Roman additions to the Primitive Creed may not be developments, arising out of a keen and vivid realising of the Divine Depositum of faith.'[1] Keble persuaded him to postpone the resignation of his living for another four months, and in September 1843 he preached in Littlemore church his last sermon as an Anglican, 'The Parting of Friends'.[2]

Newman continued to live at Littlemore, translating St Athanasius, and wrestling with two agonising accompaniments of the growing conviction that it was his duty to join the Roman Church. The first was the haunting fear that he was under an illusion, especially when men such as Keble and Pusey did not share his view. This fear could only be dispelled by waiting, by a life of penance, and by prayer and study. Four and a half hours each day were given to prayer, and nine to study and translation work. The second was the knowledge that his teaching had brought so many to the practice of a real Christian life, and that they were now thrown into confusion, and would perhaps go back, perhaps even fall into scepticism. He felt intense pain at the distress he was causing others. Friends wrote to warn him of the alarming consequences if he left the Anglican Church.

Here at home in our own communion, what confusion to our friends, what triumph to our enemies! and to Rome what an argument to confirm her in her errors and abuses! What hope, humanly speaking, can remain to our poor humbled Church, after such a blow? And now that she is beginning to show signs of life and raise her drooping head, to find herself all at once despaired of and deserted by her best champion.[3]

The year 1844 was one of 'dark night'. In September his first Oxford friend, John Bowden, died. Newman, who still believed in his Anglican Orders, gave him his Communion at the end. To leave the Church of England meant leaving so much that he

1. *Correspondence of John Henry Newman with John Keble and Others, 1839–1845*, edited at the Birmingham Oratory, London 1917, pp. 218–19
2. *S.D.*, pp. 395–409
3. *Correspondence of John Henry Newman with John Keble and Others*, p. 354

loved, and breaking with so many friends, to whom his move was incomprehensible. As he wrote to his sister Jemima at the end of December:

A person's feeling naturally is, that there must be something wrong at bottom; that I must be disappointed, or restless, or set on a theory, or carried on by a party, or coaxed into it by admirers, or influenced by any of the ten thousand persuasions which are as foreign from my mind as from my heart, but which it is easy for others to assign as an hypothesis. I do not quarrel with persons so thinking.[1]

Becoming a Catholic in England in the mid-nineteenth century had far graver social consequences than becoming a Communist in the mid-twentieth. The Catholic Church itself, as it existed in the concrete, appeared unattractive. He was driven to it only by the 'state of unbroken certainty', which he tried to treat as a dream. He wrote to Keble in November 1844, 'I am setting my face absolutely towards the wilderness', and in December:

No one can have a more unfavourable view than I of the present state of the Roman Catholics—so much so, that any who join them would be like the Cistercians of Fountains, living under trees till their house was built. If I must account for it, I should say that the want of unity has injured both them and us.[2]

As to the difficulty of the place held by the saints and our Lady in the Catholic system, and especially the honours paid to her in Italian books of devotion, which was Newman's 'great *crux* as regards Catholicism', he was helped by Dr Russell of Maynooth. From the latter he learned that some of the extreme Italian passages were omitted in English translation, which showed they were not universally acceptable. In the *Apologia* he explained how he ended by discovering that 'the Catholic Church allows no image of any sort, material or immaterial, no dogmatic symbol, no rite, no sacrament, no Saint, not even the Blessed Virgin herself, to come between the soul and its Creator. It is face to face, "solus cum solo", in all matters between man and his God'.[3] This, however, did not meet the objection that the Roman Church, in spite of its links with antiquity, had tampered with

1. *Letters and Correspondence of John Henry Newman during his Life in the English Church*, edited by Anne Mozley, II, p. 450
2. *Correspondence of John Henry Newman with John Keble and Others*, pp. 351 and 364
3. *Apo.*, p. 195

Revealed Religion and added to the Revealed truths as they were to be found in primitive times. Newman gradually became convinced that the modern Roman doctrines were legitimate developments, of which there was sufficient trace in the Early Church to recommend and prove them, on the assumption that Divine Providence was guiding the Church through the centuries. The 'Roman additions' were 'developments arising out of a keen and vivid realising of the Divine Depositum of Faith'.

At the end of 1844 Newman decided to work out fully this theory of doctrinal development in a philosophical treatise. If at the end of it his convictions in favour of the Roman Church remained, he would have to act on them.

> As I advanced, my difficulties so cleared away that I ceased to speak of 'the Roman Catholics', and boldly called them Catholics. Before I got to the end, I resolved to be received, and the book remains in the state in which it was then, unfinished.[1]

An Essay on the Development of Christian Doctrine was also intended to fulfil the duty of explaining to others the reasons for the change in his opinions. The theory of development was 'an hypothesis to account for a difficulty', the difference between the teaching of the primitive and the nineteenth-century Church. The difference was the same as that between the boy and the grown man. Newman drew out seven pragmatic tests for distinguishing legitimate developments from corruptions: fidelity to the original idea, continuity of principles, power to assimilate ideas from outside, early anticipations of later teaching, logical sequence discernible when developments were examined, preservation of earlier teaching, continuance in a state of chronic vigour. Newman said in the last pages of the book:

> When a system really is corrupt, powerful agents, when applied to it, do but develop that corruption, and bring it more speedily to an end. They stimulate it preternaturally; it puts forth its strength, and dies in some memorable act. Very different has been the history of Catholicism, when it has committed itself to such formidable influences. It has borne, and can bear, principles or doctrines, which in other systems of religion quickly degenerate into fanaticism and infidelity. This might be shown at length in the history of the Aristotelic philosophy within and without the Church; or in the history of Monachism, or of Mysticism;—not that there has not been at first a conflict between

1. *Apo.*, p. 234

these powerful and unruly elements and the Divine System into which they were entering, but that it ended in the victory of Catholicism. . . .

It is true, there have been seasons when, from the operation of external or internal causes, the Church has been thrown into what was almost a state of *deliquium*; but her wonderful revivals, while the world was triumphing over her, is a further evidence of the absence of corruption, in the system of doctrine and worship into which she has developed. . . . She pauses in her course, and almost suspends her functions; she rises again, and she is herself once more: all things are in their place and ready for action. Doctrine is where it was, and usage, and precedence, and principle, and policy; there may be changes, but they are consolidations or adaptions; all is unequivocal and determinate, with an identity which there is no disputing.[1]

Besides being an answer to his immediate problem, Newman saw a deeper and broader argument in the theory of development. Consistency is the mark of truth, and the coherent development of Christian thought was a remarkable philosophical phenomenon. As he explained in the preface to the later edition of *The Development of Doctrine*, 'the following pages were not in the first instance written to prove the divinity of the Catholic Religion, though ultimately they furnish a positive argument in its behalf'.[2] The book shows Newman's sense of history, and his theory was the result of a critical study of Patristic writings themselves, as his notebooks show. The theory was something almost entirely new, although Newman had first adumbrated it in his *Arians of the Fourth Century*, and it was accepted with very little demur in Catholic theology. It is worth noticing, too, that the *Development* was published fourteen years before Darwin's *Origin of Species*. When that book appeared, Newman found no difficulty in accepting the idea of evolution as long as it was theistic. In his Philosophical Notebook he wrote, in 1863:

There is as much want of simplicity in the idea of the creation of distinct species as in that of the creation of trees in full growth, or rocks with fossils in them. I mean that it is as strange that monkeys should be so like men, with no *historical* connection between them, as that there should be no course of facts by which fossil bones got into rocks.[3]

1. *An Essay on the Development of Christian Doctrine*, abbreviated as *Dev.*, pp. 443–4
2. *Dev.*, p. vii
3. Quoted by A. Dwight Culler, *The Imperial Intellect, A Study of Newman's Educational Ideal*, New Haven 1955, p. 267

Newman had often developed the theme of 'salvation history'. God had 'made history to be doctrine'. The Christian Revelation was not a series of propositions, but historical events, with the Incarnation at the centre. This Revelation had its own history. 'Scripture distinctly anticipates the development of Christianity, both as a polity and as a doctrine', for example, in the parable of the mustard seed. Thus the way to Christ lay through the Living Church.

It is indeed sometimes said that the stream is clearest near the spring. Whatever use may fairly be made of this image, it does not apply to the history of a philosophy or sect, which, on the contrary, is more equable, and purer, and stronger, when its bed has become deep, and broad and full. . . . In time it enters upon strange territory; points of controversy alter their bearing; parties rise and fall about it; dangers and hopes appear in new relations, and old principles appear under new forms; it changes with them in order to remain the same. In a higher world it is otherwise; but here below to live is to change, and to be perfect is to have changed often.[1]

Newman insists:

if Christianity be a universal religion, suited not to one locality or period, but to all times and places, it cannot but vary in its relations and dealings towards the world around it, that is, it will develop. Principles require a very various application according to persons and circumstances, and must be thrown into new shapes according to the form of society which they are to influence. Hence all bodies of Christians, orthodox or not, develop the doctrines of Scripture.[2]

These last sentences have caused the *Essay on Development* to be described as a handbook of missionary adaptation, and the later pages on the power of Christianity to assimilate ideas from outside justify the title. The conclusion Newman drew was the 'probability of a Developing Authority in Christianity'.

Relying on his palmary argument from 'antecedent probability', he urged that a Revelation from God given in history required a living authority in every age, guaranteed to keep it immune from error. 'Some authority there must be if there is a revelation, and other authority there is none but' the Church, which 'Scripture expressly calls "the pillar and ground of Truth"'. 'Surely, either an objective revelation has not been given, or it has been provided

1. *Dev.*, pp. 73 and 40   2. *Dev.*, pp. 58

with means for impressing its objectiveness on the world.' 'If Christianity is both social and dogmatic, and intended for all ages, it must, humanly speaking, have an infallible expounder.'[1]

As an Anglican Newman had appealed to Antiquity—the faith of the ancient Church before it split into branches, was the source of truth—'My bulwark was the Fathers'. Although he now recognised that there must be a living present authority in the Church, his principle still held: that Church was the Church of Christ which was historically the successor of the Church of the Fathers. Christ had left behind Him a Divine Society. That Society, which existed in ancient times, could not fail. It must exist now, and—final step—the Roman Church was identical with the Church of the Fathers. On 8 October 1845 Newman wrote to Pusey that he was about to be received 'into what I believe to be the one and only fold of the Redeemer'. Newman was always unwilling to put into words his reasons for becoming a Catholic. 'Catholicism is a deep matter—you cannot take it up in a teacup.' 'People shall not say, "We have now got his reasons and know their worth".'[2]

Eventually he gave to the world his *Apologia*, and later, in 1874, commenting on his essay 'The Catholicity of the Anglican Church', in which he tried to lay the ghost he had seen in the summer of 1839, he wrote:

> I was always asking myself what would the Fathers have done, what would those whose works were around my room, whose names were ever meeting my eyes, whose authority was ever influencing my judgment, what would these men have said, how would they have acted in my position? I had made a good case for Anglicanism on paper, but what judgment would be passed on it by Athanasius, Basil, Gregory, Hilary, and Ambrose? The more I considered the matter, the more I thought that these Fathers, if they examined the antagonist pleas, would give it against me.[3]

Newman proceeded to quote a passage whose rhetoric must not blind us to the critical and minute historical research on which it was based.

> I expressed this feeling in my Essay on the Development of Christian Doctrine. 'Did St Athanasius, or St Ambrose come suddenly to life,

1. *Dev.*, pp. 88–90
2. *L. and D.*, XI, p. 110
3. *Essays Critical and Historical* II, pp. 74–5

it cannot be doubted,' I said ironically, 'what communion they would mistake for their own. All surely will agree that these Fathers, with whatever differences of opinion, whatever protests, if we will, would find themselves more at home with such men as St Bernard, or St Ignatius Loyola, or with the lonely priest in his lodgings, or the holy sisterhood of Charity, or the unlettered crowd before the altar, than with the rulers or members of any other religious community. And may we not add, that were the two Saints, who once sojourned in exile or on embassage at Treves, to come more northward still, and to travel until they reached another fair city, seated among groves, green meadows, and calm streams, the holy brothers would turn from many a high aisle and solemn cloister which they found there, and ask the way to some small chapel, where mass was said, in the populous alley or the forlorn suburb? And, on the other hand, can any one who has but heard his name, and cursorily read his history, doubt for one instant, how the people of England, in turn, . . . would deal with Athanasius,—Athanasius, who spent his long years in fighting against kings for a theological term?[1]

Newman added:

I recommend this passage to the consideration of those more than friendly critics of mine, who, in their perplexity to find a motive sufficient for my becoming a Catholic, attribute the step to me personally . . . to a desire for a firmer ground of religious certainty, and a clearer view of revealed truth, than is furnished in the Church of England.

That was a body separate from the Roman Church, and for him it was a grave duty, if he was to be obedient to Revealed Religion, to enter what he held to be 'the One Church of the Redeemer'. Thus it was that at the end of his *Apologia* he could write:

I was not conscious to myself, on my conversion, of any change, intellectual or moral, wrought in my mind. I was not conscious of firmer faith in the fundamental truths of Revelation, or of more self-command; I had not more fervour; but it was like coming into port after a rough sea.[2]

Newman did not reject his past. The step he now took was to him a mere corollary of the conversion by which he gave himself to God at the age of sixteen.

In spite of the prolonged and violent Protestant reaction in the Church of England against the Tractarians, the opposition of the bishops and the great body of the Church, Newman certainly

1. *Dev.*, pp. 97–8 2. *Apo.*, p. 238

realised, as his letters show, that 'Catholic' views were slowly making headway. It is sometimes asked whether he would not have done better to remain in Anglicanism and catholicise it, (which was what his enemies accused him of doing), and thus perhaps have prepared the way for unity. This was impossible, when his conscience told him that the Church of England was in schism, and that he could not be saved outside the Roman Church. If he had stayed in Anglicanism, he might have worked against the bishops to catholicise it, but he would have lost his integrity, and with it ultimately his influence. Pusey, who could not accept Newman's step, had a very generous explanation in the opposite direction. In a letter that appeared in the *English Churchman* on 16 October 1845, he wrote:

> . . . Our Church has not known how to employ him. And since this was so, it seemed as if a sharp sword were lying in its scabbard, or hung up in the sanctuary because there was no one to wield it. . . . He is gone unconscious (as all great instruments of God are) what he himself is. He has gone as a simple act of duty with no view for himself, placing himself entirely in God's hands. And such are they whom God employs. He seems to me not so much gone from us, as transplanted into another part of the Vineyard, where the full energies of his powerful mind can be employed, which here they were not. And who knows what in the mysterious purposes of God's good Providence may be the effect of such a person among them? You too have felt that it is what is unholy on both sides which keeps us apart. It is not what is true in the Roman system, against which the strong feeling of ordinary religious people among us is directed, but against what is unholy in her practice. It is not anything in our Church which keeps them from acknowledging us, but heresy existing more or less within us. . . . It is perhaps the greatest event which has happened since the Communion of the Churches has been interrupted, that such an one, so formed in our Church, and the work of God's Spirit as dwelling within her, should be transplanted to theirs. If anything could open their eyes to what is good in us, or soften in us any wrong prejudices against them, it would be the presence of such an one, nurtured and grown to such ripeness in our Church, and now removed to theirs.[1]

James Hope consoled Gladstone in the same way: 'Pray remember the beneficial effect which the English mind will thereby bring to bear upon the Roman Church itself.'

1. Quoted in H. P. Liddon, *Life of Edward Bouverie Pusey*, London 1894, II, p. 461

Dean Church, like Pusey, one of Newman's closest friends, had his explanation too, and a noble one, even though it does not altogether tally with Newman's. Two days after the latter's death, he wrote:

Is not the ultimate key to Newman's history his keen and profound sense of the life, society, and principles of action presented in the New Testament? . . . The English Church had exchanged religion for civilisation, the first century for the nineteenth . . . it was all very well, but it was not the Christianity of the New Testament and of the first ages. . . . Alas! there was nothing completely like them; but of all unlike things, the Church of England with its 'smug parsons', and pony-carriages for their wives and daughters, seemed to him the most unlike: more unlike than the great unreformed Roman Church, with its strange unscriptural doctrines and its undeniable crimes, and its alliance, wherever it could, with the world. But at least the Roman Church had not only preserved, but maintained at full strength through the centuries to our day two things of which the New Testament was full, and which are characteristic of it—devotion and self-sacrifice. . . . Devotion and sacrifice, prayer and self-denying charity, in one word sanctity, are at once on the surface of the New Testament and interwoven with all its substance. He recoiled from a representation of the religion of the New Testament which to his eye was without them. He turned to where, in spite of every other disadvantage, he thought he found them. In S. Filippo Neri he could find a link between the New Testament and progressive civilisation. He could find no S. Filippo—so modern and yet so scriptural—when he sought at home.[1]

As has been seen, Newman, on the contrary, warned men of the danger of looking to the Roman Church as the place where greater encouragement was to be had in the search for holiness, and in 1879 he was still warning people of this danger, and against joining it 'merely because they can pray better in it, or have more fervency than in the Anglican Church'. Then, too, Dean Church seems to underestimate Newman's appreciation of things Anglican, for which there is such continual evidence. To Isaac Williams Newman wrote in 1863: 'Of all human things, perhaps Oxford is dearest to my heart, and some parsonages in the country.' And in 1877 he made an entry at the end of his Philosophical Notebook about his love for his 'active abidance in time past in the Church of England', and how he delighted to look at the photograph of the interior of Trinity Chapel on the wall of his room:

1. *Occasional Papers*, London 1897, II, pp. 470–4

Yet it is not the Church of England that I love—but it is that very assemblage, in its individuals concrete, which I remember so well—the scenes, occurrences, my own thoughts, feelings, and acts. I look at that communion table and recollect with what feelings I went up to it in November 1817 for my first communion.

To leave Anglicanism was painful in the extreme. It meant leaving all the things he loved best, it meant breaking with most of his friends and with his own family. Pusey continued to write, but the correspondence with Keble and Church petered out, and they and so many others kept aloof for twenty years.

CHAPTER 6

The English Oratory: the Irish University (1846-58)

NEWMAN was received into the Church of Rome, at Littlemore, by Fr Dominic Barberi, an Italian Passionist from Viterbo, on 9 October 1845. They had met once before. In the summer of 1844 Fr Dominic, who was giving a mission in Oxfordshire, paid a visit to Littlemore. When his second visit was imminent Newman described him to Mrs Bowden:

He was a poor boy, who (I believe) kept sheep near Rome and from his youth his thoughts have been most singularly and distinctly turned to the conversion of England. He is a shrewd clever man, but as unaffected and simple as a child; and most singularly kind in his thoughts of religious persons in our communion. I wish all persons were as charitable as I know him to be. After waiting near thirty years, suddenly his superiors sent him to England, without any act of his own. However, he has not laboured in conversions, but confined himself to missions and retreats among his own people. I believe him to be a very holy man.[1]

Fr Dominic was declared blessed by Paul VI in 1963. The instrument of the first and fundamental conversion, 'the human means of the beginning of divine faith' in Newman, had been Walter Mayers, but the second conversion was the work of no human instrument. Although Bishop Wiseman and Dr Russell had their parts to play, mere human pressures, however charitably meant, could only have done harm, as Newman explained in the *Apologia*.

There was nothing, indeed, at the time more likely to throw me back. 'Why do you meddle? why cannot you let me alone? You can do me no good; you know nothing on earth about me; you may actually do me harm; I am in better hands than yours.'[2]

Two of Newman's friends became Catholics with him, a considerable number had preceded him, and in the next few years

1. *L. and D.*, XI, pp. 5–6　　2. *Apo.*, p. 126

several hundred University and educated men followed his example, no longer able to accept 'the Catholicity of the Anglican Church'. 'Through the autumn and the next year,' wrote Dean Church, 'friends whose names and forms were familiar in Oxford, one by one disappeared and were lost to it. Fellowships, livings, curacies, intended careers were given up.' He adds: 'a considerable portion of English society learned what it was to be novices in a religious system, hitherto not only alien and unknown, but dreaded, or else to have lost friends and relatives, who were suddenly transformed into severe and uncompromising opponents.'[1] As for Newman, he now began a second life, in a different world. A second life, because he had already lived a life and enjoyed a career, a success and a fame that many men might envy—a different world, because he was leaving the main-stream of English society, and entering a rivulet, a minority group, just recovering from restrictions, educationally backward, and still for the most part composed either of aristocratic and landed families with their dependents, or poor Irish immigrants in the large cities. Yet in a sense Newman changed very little. The new beliefs he now accepted were peripheral and comparatively unimportant. He did not have to alter his doctrine on the Church, but now acknowledged the Catholic Church of his day as that of St Ambrose and St Athanasius. On its authority he accepted the papal prerogatives. He had long believed and taught most earnestly the doctrine of the real presence, he now added to it that of transubstantiation, thinking it to be included in the Church's teaching. But he knew that the reality of Christ's presence in the Holy Eucharist could not be adequately explained in words, and exclaimed: 'What do I know of substance or matter? just as much as the greatest philosophers, and that is nothing at all.' He accepted the doctrine of purgatory, indulgences and the invocation of saints. Belief in their intercession had always been an Anglican doctrine. As to our Lady, Newman was able to state in the *Apologia*: 'I had a true devotion to the Blessed Virgin, in whose College I lived, whose Altar I served, and whose Immaculate Purity I had in one of my earliest sermons made much of.'[2] His devotion to Revealed Religion was unchanged, and this was what gave his life its unity. His lifelong principles, about the

1. R. W. Church, *The Oxford Movement*, pp. 394–5
2. *Apo.*, pp. 239–40, 165. See above, p. 29

supremacy of conscience, about the way to certitude in matters of faith, about the concrete and personal approach in the religious as in other spheres, as well as his scriptural and patristic theology were carried over into the new world. In matters of prayer and devotion, although he added Catholic practices such as the Rosary and visits to the Blessed Sacrament, he still kept to the formulas of his youth. The early prayers he had composed or adapted after his conversion, were copied out again in the booklets he read, to the end of his life, during his thanksgiving after Mass. The very intentions, particularised, of his prayers, he continued to use almost unchanged.

One alteration in himself Newman described graphically in his note on the Anglican Church at the end of the *Apologia*.

I said, in a former page, that, on my conversion, I was not conscious of any change in me of thought or feeling, as regards matters of doctrine; this, however, was not the case as regards some matters of fact, and, unwilling as I am to give offence to religious Anglicans, I am bound to confess that I felt a great change in my view of the Church of England. I cannot tell how soon there came on me,—but very soon,—an extreme astonishment that I had ever imagined it to be a portion of the Catholic Church. For the first time I looked at it from without, and (as I should myself say) saw it as it was . . . a mere national institution. As if my eyes were suddenly opened, so I saw it—spontaneously, apart from any definite act of reason or any argument; and so I have seen it ever since. I suppose, the main cause of this lay in the contrast which was presented to me by the Catholic Church. Then I recognized at once a reality which was quite a new thing with me. Then I was sensible that I was not making for myself a Church by an effort of thought; I needed not to make an act of faith in her; I had not painfully to force myself into a position, but my mind fell back upon itself in relaxation and in peace, and I gazed at her almost passively, as a great objective fact. I looked at her;—at her rites, her ceremonial, and her precepts; and I said, 'This *is* a religion'; and then, when I looked back upon the poor Anglican Church, for which I had laboured so hard, and upon all that appertained to it, and thought of our various attempts to dress it up doctrinally and esthetically, it seemed to me to be the veriest of nonentities.

Newman added that he regarded it, nevertheless, as 'a great national organ, a source of vast popular advantage, and, to a certain point, a witness and teacher of religious truth'.[1]

1. *Apo.*, pp. 339–40

Once a Catholic, Newman insisted, 'we must throw ourselves into the system'. He left Littlemore in February 1846 and remained for a few months outside Birmingham, at Old Oscott, near the College over which Wiseman presided. At the old college he collected some of the converts who had lived with him at Littlemore, and in September left with one of them, the faithful Ambrose St John, for Rome. There they went to the College of Propaganda for the study of theology. Newman was, if anything too humble and docile. Purely optional things, such as the prayers for gaining indulgences, worried him, and he thought it necessary to take over some of the exaggerated Catholic devotion to our Lady, impelled not by the old Catholics but by the enthusiastic young converts around him. Before long he fell back on the sober advice given him by English Vicars-Apostolic, as the Catholic bishops were called, and on his natural preference for English habits of belief and devotion. He was at once struck by the simplicity and the objective sense of spiritual realities that he found among Catholics. Yet he was not uncritical. He noted the absence of any real philosophy in the Roman schools, and the cut and dried teaching. 'There is an iron form here.' To his sister Jemima he wrote of the Romans: 'One is struck at once with their horrible cruelty to animals—also with their dishonesty, lying and stealing apparently without any conscience,' this with 'a simple certainty in believing which to a Protestant or Anglican is quite astounding . . . they show in a wonderful way how it is possible to disjoin religion and morality'. Of course, there was much that was good as well, although among the more educated there was 'a deep suspicion of *change*, with a perfect incapacity to create anything *positive* for the wants of the times'.[1]

In Rome Newman had to settle his vocation and that of the small group who wished to throw in their lot with him. He considered joining various religious orders, but realised that his previous life was intended to be the means of future usefulness. To J. D. Dalgairns, one of his followers, he wrote: 'My name and person are known to a very great many people I do not know—so are my books—and I may have begun a work which I am now to finish.' As a religious or Jesuit 'no one would know that I was speaking my own words: or was a *continuation*, as it were, of my former self'.[2] This was one of the advantages of the Oratory of

1. *L. and D.*, XII, pp. 24 and 104

2. *L. and D.*, XI, p. 306

St Philip Neri, which Wiseman had favoured from the first. St Philip had founded in the sixteenth century in Rome, not a new order, but a group of secular priests, who lived together without taking vows, and with 'no bond but that of love'. Each house of the Oratory lived its own separate democratic life, and must be situated with its church in a town. From there its influence was to radiate, by its services and preaching, teaching, study and learned work. Newman was attracted by St Philip at once, and later described him:

He would be but an ordinary individual priest as others: and his weapons should be but unaffected humility and unpretending love. All he did was to be done by the light, and fervour, and convincing eloquence of his personal character and his easy conversation.[1]

To Jemima, Newman wrote:

This great saint reminds me in so many ways of Keble, that I can fancy what Keble would have been, if God's will had been that he should have been born in another place or age; he was formed in the same type of extreme hatred of humbug, playfulness, nay oddity, tender love for others, and serenity, which are the lineaments of Keble.[2]

The Oratorians were free subjects, who had few rules and must learn to live together by means of tact, self-knowledge and the knowledge of others. Each had his own work and was to rely on personal influence rather than discipline in pursuing it. This was Newman's way, and the fact that he and his companions had learned to live together at Littlemore and old Oscott meant that their work of preparation was already half done. Pius IX gave him authority to establish Oratories in England, and allowed him to adapt and bring up to date St Philip's Rule for the purpose. During his training in Oratorian ways in Rome Newman made an intensive study of the history and spirit of St Philip and his institute. He did not mean to reproduce a slavish model of the Italian Oratory, but to realise most faithfully St Philip's *idea* in very different circumstances. He was appointed Superior of the first foundation, which was to be in Birmingham, where Wiseman was Vicar Apostolic. This first house was set up at Old Oscott, rechristened Maryvale, on 1 February 1848, the eve of the Purification, which was the feast of St Mary's College, Oriel, at Oxford. Shortly afterwards, at Wiseman's wish, and against his own

1. *The Idea of a University*, abbreviated as *Idea*, p. 236
2. *L. and D.*, XII, p. 25

judgment, Newman admitted as novices to the Oratory another convert group, headed by the emotional and exuberant Frederick William Faber. Early in 1849 Newman moved to Alcester Street in the middle of Birmingham, where the Oratory and a church were established with a parish and schools. He devoted himself to work among the poor, who included many with practically no knowledge of the Christian faith, and many immigrants, Irish men and women driven to England by the Famine. In April he founded a second house of the Oratory in London, putting Faber in charge.

It would be hard to exaggerate the importance of the Oratory for Newman. It was his chosen vocation; to found it in England was the first commission he received from the Catholic authorities; it was the framework for the rest of his long life, and, as has so often been the case with founders, through it some of his cruellest trials came. He only succeeded in founding two Oratories, although he had hoped for many more. Faber took with him to London Newman's prestige, but, especially after the London house became independent in 1853, it developed on different lines. One of the effects of the secessions from Anglicanism was that the converts, who beforehand had regarded Newman as their leader, now began to feel that they were all neophytes together, all on a level and that they could be as good or better Catholics than he. They became extremists, and as time went on were ready to look down on him as a 'Gallican', or 'only half a Catholic'. It is a curious fact that almost all those who were to oppose Newman were converts, while the 'old Catholics' were to be among his staunchest supporters. There was a similar phenomenon among the Oratorians in London. Although most of them owed their new allegiance and their religious vocation to him and all were much his juniors in age, they began to feel they were better Oratorians or truer sons of St Philip than he. Newman remained English and moderate, they tended to be Italianate and extreme ultramontane exalters of the papacy. The breach between the two Oratories came in 1855, when Newman asked the London house to rectify in Rome what he considered to be a grave misunderstanding they had created about the Oratorian Rule he had brought to England. This they refused to do; they were hurt by his manner, and began to spread about their version of the affair. If the disagreement had remained private, scandal would have been avoided. Newman himself kept silent and made his own

Oratorians do the same. He felt that he could not defend himself without disparaging Faber. And Faber, although he alienated many English people by his Italian extravagance (perhaps even, some would hazard, spoiled a golden opportunity), by his personality and his writings exercised a wide influence for good, which must not be jeopardised. But for Newman the difference was one of principle, involving the stability of his institute, and to this position he held, without justifying himself in face of the injurious gossip of which he was well aware.

In 1849 these trials lay in the future, and his first years as a Catholic were a period when Newman relaxed and blossomed out after the long agony of his 'Anglican deathbed'. There were the pains of acclimatisation, it is true, and all the harassment of founding the two Oratorian houses, but he was at peace and full of confidence and energy. While in Rome he wrote his first novel, *Loss and Gain*, about an Oxford convert, the amusing reply to a story, *From Oxford to Rome*, by a Miss Harris, which was having a great success in England. Newman's hero belongs to the younger generation of Oxford Tractarians, so that only occasionally is the story autobiographical. But the atmosphere of Oxford is reproduced, and the arguments about faith, and conversion and the Church enlivened by humour and irony. Pusey is mentioned with esteem and Newman is Smith, 'he never speaks decidedly on difficult questions'. One recent Newman anthology has included this vivid story entire.

Then amid the poor at Alcester Street, Newman preached and wrote his first volume of Catholic sermons, *Discourses addressed to Mixed Congregations*. These are much more elaborate and ornate than the Anglican sermons, and contain many passages of eloquent beauty, although there was nothing above the head of his mixed audience. They are genuine Newman, but not typical. In his docility, he was basing himself on Catholic models. He warned his hearers to live up to the beliefs they professed and was criticised as stern. Faber saw in the sermons 'a determinate effort to lift up the old Catholic tone and standard'.

Newman's sermons also impressed a very different person, Edward Burne-Jones, then at King Edward's School, Birmingham. In later life he put into words the memories of his youth:

When I was fifteen or sixteen he taught me so much I do mind—things that will never be out of me. In an age of sofas and cushions he taught me to be indifferent to comfort; and in an age of materialism he taught me to venture all on the unseen, and this so early that it was well in me when life began, and I was equipped before I went to Oxford with a really good panoply, and it has never failed me; so that if this world cannot tempt me with money and luxury, and it can't, or honours or anything it has in its trumpery treasure-house, it is most of all because he said it in a way that touched me—not scolding nor forbidding nor much leading—walking with me a step in front. . . . I wanted to go to Oxford because of him, but when I got there, I saw nothing like what I had left in the grimy streets of Birmingham.[1]

Discourses to Mixed Congregations was not the only volume of sermons Newman published in 1849. The fourth volume of his *Parochial Sermons* was out of print, and he brought out a new edition, with various alterations intended to make it acceptable to Catholics. This he did in deference to the strong opinion of Charles Newsham, President of Ushaw College, Durham. The edition was a failure. People wanted Newman unexpurgated. From the alterations, Newman thought it wise to make, something is to be learned. A few of the changes were obvious ones—the distinction between mortal and venial sin was made clear, phrases connected with the Holy Eucharist such as 'the Lord's table' were altered, and references to confession and the invocation of saints introduced. But as to the doctrine of the Presence of God in the soul, the Indwelling, which he had preached so clearly in St Mary's, the great passages were still there. Newman retracted nothing of that: how could he? Yet in a few places there were curious tonings down, which suggest that he felt the teaching and language of Scripture and the Fathers to be not altogether in tune with the ethos of the Church in the reign of Pius IX. Thus: (1) 'Let us come to the ordinances of grace, in which Christ gives His holy Spirit' has been changed to 'Let us come where He gives grace, let us come to His holy Church in which Christ vouchsafes to dwell'.[2] (2) 'He [Christ] came again in the Person of His Spirit' is altered to 'He gave them the gifts of the Spirit'.[3] (3) 'We have been . . . brought into that . . . mysterious Presence of God . . . which is in us and around us, and is in our heart,' is changed to 'brought under that mysterious Power of God'.[4] (4) Newman

1. Frances Horner, *Times Remembered*, London 1933, p. 120
2. *P.S.*, IV, p. 17
3. *P.S.*, IV, p. 169
4. *P.S.*, IV, p. 229

speaks of those who came close to our Lord externally, his executioners, the beloved disciple: 'His Blessed Mother, indeed, came closer still to Him; and we, if we be but true believers, still closer, who have him really though spiritually within us; but this is another, an inward sort of approach.' Here the reference to the Indwelling is removed and the sense completely altered, no doubt to avoid any apparent slight to our Lady. It reads: 'His Blessed Mother, indeed, came closer still to Him; but this is another, an inward sort of approach.'[1] Yet the Fathers praised our Lady, because *prius concepit mente quam corpore*. (5) Our Lord's Presence in us is turned into a reference to the Blessed Eucharist. 'The Presence of the Eternal Son, ten times more glorious, more powerful than when He trod the earth in our flesh, is with us,' has become '. . . trod the earth, is in His sacred tabernacle still'.[2] That reminds us of what modern Roman theologians have written as to a wrong emphasis in devotion to the reserved Sacrament. This has been given us primarily as our sacrifice and as the food of our communion. Newman showed a great devotion to the Blessed Sacrament reserved, but did not allow this to distract him from the Real Presence of Christ within us, which the Holy Eucharist is supremely intended to foster.[3] However, as we have seen, he realised that things were at a somewhat low ebb, intellectually and spiritually in the Roman Church, when he entered it. In his *Development of Doctrine* he even made this into a mark of the Church:

If then there is now a form of Christianity such that . . . its members are degenerate and corrupt, and surpassed in conscientiousness and in virtue, as in gifts of intellect, by the very heretics it condemns . . . such a religion is not unlike the Christianity of the fifth and sixth Centuries.[4]

In 1850 the Gorham Case confirmed all that Newman had felt about the Erastianism of the Anglican Church, and caused great controversy and excitement. The Bishop of Exeter refused to institute the Reverend G. C. Gorham to the Vicarage of Bramford

1. *P.S.*, IV, p. 247 2. *P.S.*, IV, p. 265
3. Among other evidence the prayers to the Holy Spirit in the posthumously published *Meditations on Christian Doctrine* show how Newman's devotion to the Indwelling Spirit continued undiminished to the end of his life. It should be noted, too, that he prayed regularly before the Blessed Sacrament, sometimes for long periods at a time.
4. *Dev.*, p. 322.

Speke, on the ground that his views on baptismal regeneration were unsound. The Judicial Committee of the Privy Council decided that Gorham's views were not contrary to the teaching of the Church of England and he was able to take over his living. The decision emphasised the Church's dependence on the State and led to a further wave of conversions, which included many of Newman's friends such as James Hope, Henry Edward Manning and Robert Wilberforce, who all became Catholics in 1851. Before their conversion Newman was persuaded that it was his duty to win over the Tractarians, 'the children of the Oxford Movement', who, if they were true to the principles he had taught them, ought now at least to follow him out of Anglicanism. In the summer of 1850 he delivered a series of lectures at the Oratory in London, then situated in King William Street, near Charing Cross. They were published after delivery as *Certain Difficulties felt by Anglicans in submitting to the Catholic Church,* (later altered to *in Catholic Teaching*). From the literary point of view this was one of Newman's most perfect works, although written more 'intellectually against the grain' than anything else of his. His mind had been full of its subject since 1841. He always insisted that in writing it he was not acting in direct hostility to the Anglican Church as such, but merely carrying the Oxford Movement to its legitimate conclusion. He argued that the Movement was foreign to the National Church and did not derive its life from it. It's 'idea or first principle was ecclesiastical liberty; the doctrine which it especially opposed was in ecclesiastical language, the heresy of Erastus, and in political, the Royal Supremacy', Newman said in the fourth lecture; and added:

> When I thus represent the idea of the movement of which I am speaking, I must not be supposed to overlook or deny to it its theological, or its ritual, or its practical aspect; but I am speaking of what may be called its *form* . . . the writers of the Apostolical party of 1833 were earnest and copious in their enforcement of the high doctrines of the faith, of dogmatism, of the sacramental principle . . . and of the counsels of perfection; but, considering all those great articles of teaching to be protected and guaranteed by the independence of the Church.[1]

Newman showed powerfully the extent to which the Anglican Church depended on the State, but the lesson of history has been

1. *Diff.*, I, pp. 101–2

that he exaggerated, or rather that, thanks to Tractarianism, it later won greater independence. He willingly admitted the spiritual gifts and graces among Anglicans, and spoke of his own past:

Can I forget,—I never can forget,—the day when in my youth I first bound myself to the ministry of God in that old church of St Frideswide, the patroness of Oxford? nor how I wept most abundant, and most sweet tears, when I thought what I had then become; though I looked on ordination as no sacramental rite, nor even to baptism ascribed any supernatural virtue? Can I wipe from my memory, or wish to wipe out, those happy Sunday mornings, light or dark, year after year, when I celebrated your communion-rite, in my own church of St. Mary's, and in the pleasantness and joy of it heard nothing of the strife of tongues which surrounded its walls?[1]

In the fifth lecture Newman showed how the Oxford Movement was built on submission to the authorities of the Church, the bishops, nearly all of whom 'gladly availed themselves of the power conferred on them by the movement against the movement itself. They fearlessly handselled their Apostolic weapons upon the Apostolic party'.[2]

In the later lectures Newman dealt with objections on the Catholic side, notably one very pressing in those days, the 'backwardness of Catholic Countries'. R. H. Hutton described the lectures, at which he was present:

Never did a voice seem better adapted to persuade without irritating. Singularly sweet, perfectly free from any dictatorial note, and yet rich in all the cadences proper to the expression of pathos, of wonder, and of ridicule, there was still nothing in it that any one could properly describe as insinuating, for its simplicity, and frankness, and freedom from the half-smothered notes which express indirect purpose, was as remarkable as its sweetness, its freshness, and its gentle distinctness.[3]

Difficulties of Anglicans had barely been published when Cardinal Wiseman's clumsy announcement, in October 1850, of the setting up of a Catholic territorial hierarchy in place of Vicars-Apostolic sparked off the violent 'Papal Aggression' agitation. It is difficult to realise the fury aroused. Protest meetings were held all over England, the Pope and Wiseman were burnt in effigy, and Newman himself was one of the chief targets. Addresses were sent

1. *Diff.*, I, pp. 81–2
2. *Diff.*, I, p. 152
3. R. H. Hutton, *Cardinal Newman*, London 1891, pp. 207–8

to the Queen, the Prime Minister Lord John Russell denounced the insolent and insidious aggression of Pius IX, and an Ecclesiastical Titles Bill against the new sees was passed into law. The agitation showed the strength of English Protestantism. Anglican bishops and clergy played a leading part in directing the popular fury. Catholics feared for a new period of persecution, although perhaps the most bitter insults were reserved for the Tractarians who had remained Anglican, the Puseyites. Newman thought the hierarchy a mistake and doubted whether enough suitable men could be found to fill all the new sees. From the time he joined his new communion he realised that its greatest weakness in England was the low intellectual standard. There was no centre of critical and alert theology. He had hoped to begin something himself, but in Rome soon discovered that for a convert this would not be possible. In August 1850 he wrote to Rome to Mgr Talbot (who, with Wiseman, was immediately responsible for the new hierarchy), 'I suppose our most crying want is the want of theology', and wondered whether Pius IX could not send theologians to England as his predecessor had sent St Theodore and St Adrian. Now in the midst of all the agitation Newman exclaimed: 'We want theology, not bishops.' But once the deed had been done, he was for braving the storm and not yielding an inch. The Church was not merely the hierarchy but all the People of God, and the Catholics themselves must stand up for their rights. 'I dare say it may be advisable for our Bishops to do nothing—but for that reason, if for no other, the laity should stir.' He approved of the plan of his friend, J. M. Capes, for Catholic lectures by laymen in every large town. Of Ullathorne, his own bishop at Birmingham, Newman wrote: 'He has a horror of laymen, and I am sure that they may be made in this day the strength of the Church.'[1] Fortunately Wiseman approved and the lectures were delivered. Newman himself took a hand in Birmingham, and produced what he called his best-written work, *Lectures on the Present Position of Catholics in England.* It was a sustained attack on that fanatical Protestant view of the Church which led to such unjust consequences. Chesterton described it as having been practically preached to a raging mob. It is full of humour and irony, but these are employed in strict subservience to the main purpose. 'In my lectures on Catholicism in England,'

1. *L. and D.*, XIV, pp. 35, 216, 252

Newman wrote later, 'I oppose, not the Anglican Church, but National Protestantism, and Anglicans only so far as they belong to it'.[1] At the time, he objected to Capes's attacks on the Establishment, which was a bulwark against unbelief and protected the faith of so many:

I still shrink from taking your line of attacking the Church of England. I ask 'could we supply the place of it and all sects?' See, we have not priests enough for our own body—how much less for England. Besides, I think our game is *not* to return evil for evil, now that the parsons have attacked us so furiously.[2]

Lectures on Catholics in England concludes with an appeal to the laity:

Your strength lies in your God and your conscience; therefore it lies not in your number. It lies not in your number any more than in intrigue, or combination or worldly wisdom. . . . What I desiderate in Catholics is the gift of bringing out what their religion is. . . . I want a laity, not arrogant, not rash in speech, not disputatious, but men who know their religion, who enter into it, who know just where they stand, who know what they hold and what they do not, who know their creed so well that they can give an account of it, who know so much of history that they can defend it. I want an intelligent, well-instructed laity; I am not denying you are such already: but I mean to be severe, and, as some would say, exorbitant in my demands, I wish you to enlarge your knowledge, to cultivate your reason, to get an insight into the relation of truth to truth, to learn to view things as they are, to understand how faith and reason stand to each other, what are the bases and principles of Catholicism, and where lie the main inconsistencies and absurdities of the Protestant theory. I have no apprehension that you will be the worse Catholics for familiarity with these subjects, provided you cherish a vivid sense of God above, and keep in mind that you have souls to be judged and saved. In all times the laity have been the measure of the Catholic spirit; they saved the Irish Church three centuries ago, and they betrayed the Church in England.[3]

One of the weaknesses of the Church was its clericalisation and the consequent inferior position of the laity. This Newman, who had learned from the source of revelation that the Church was not merely the clergy but all who had received the Holy

1. *Ward*, II, p. 57 2. *L. and D.*, XIV, p. 207
3. *Lectures on the Present Position of Catholics in England*, pp. 388–91

Spirit, realised keenly. It was a deviation he tried to remedy. There was one aspect of it which touched his heart. He welcomed the plan for lay lecturers in 1850 because, as he wrote at the time, 'It has fretted me, ever since I was a Catholic, that so little use was made of the married converts, like Anglican clergymen, who, I have said and truly, viewed together have an amount of talent, which the unmarried clergy converted have not'.[1] These married convert clergy found themselves treated as laymen. They experienced difficulty in finding suitable work and even in earning their living. There was talk of giving them 'Minor Orders' which would have enabled them at least to preach sermons, but nothing came of this, and the unique opportunity provided by a non-recurring influx of talent was missed.

One consequence of the *Lectures on the Present Position of Catholics* was that Newman was involved in a trial for libel. In the fifth lecture he had denounced the ex-Dominican Giacinto Achilli, from the Papal States, who was enthralling audiences with his accounts of the corruptions of Rome and his own sufferings for his beliefs at the hands of the Inquisition. He was sponsored by The Evangelical Alliance, which had been founded in London in 1846 'to associate and concentrate the strength of an enlightened Protestantism against the encroachments of Popery and Puseyism, and to promote the interests of a Scriptural Christianity'. In fact Achilli had been in trouble for a series of crimes of seduction. Cardinal Wiseman had already shown him up in the *Dublin Review*, and had documentary proof of the often very scandalous crimes. Relying on this, and in order to undermine his reliability as a witness, Newman denounced Achilli, who had lectured in Birmingham and had impressed even Catholics by what appeared to be the testimony of actual experience. Unfortunately Wiseman failed to produce his vital documents, which might have staved off a trial, and Newman spent a harassing eighteen months under the threat of a term of imprisonment. He was able to bring to England as witnesses some of Achilli's victims, respectable married women, and secured a moral victory. But, since he could not substantiate every charge, he was found guilty of libel, and fined £100. Judges and jury were biased, and it was recognised that Protestant prejudice had led to a miscarriage of justice. Newman's expenses, £12,000, were paid by

1. *L. and D.*, XIV, pp. 98–9

Catholics from all over the world, but in the eyes of the English public he was somewhat disgraced.

In the midst of these anxieties Newman was asked by the Irish bishops to found a Catholic University in Dublin. Their immediate aim was to provide an alternative to the Queen's Colleges which Peel had established in Ireland. These had been rejected on the ground that all religious teaching was excluded from them and that they were 'mixed', open to members of all Churches and none. Religious tests were still in force at Oxford and Cambridge, and the proposal was that the new university should provide for the needs of the English-speaking world, and resemble the Catholic University which the Belgian bishops had recently re-established in Louvain. It was a great opportunity to provide for the higher education of the laity, which to Newman was of such importance. He hoped also that it would be a meeting-ground for clergy and laity, and enable them to work together. He agreed to give several years to launching the University, provided he received permission from Pius IX to be absent from his Oratory at Birmingham (newly installed in the house he had built for it at Edgbaston) for such periods each year as the task required. As a preparatory step, Archbishop Cullen of Armagh, soon to become Archbishop of Dublin, asked Newman to deliver lectures in the latter city, on the harm of 'mixed' education, and on the Catholic view of what university education should be. Cullen, whose life had until that time been spent at the Irish College in Rome, had a rather different idea of a university from Newman's. This did not make any easier the latter's task of combining in one series of lectures a discussion of the evils of education without religion and of the nature of university education in itself.

Newman delivered five of the *Discourses on the Nature and Scope of University Education* in Dublin during May 1852, and published them with five more later in the year. With certain alterations and omissions of ephemeral matter, they now form the first part of *The Idea of a University*. All his Oxford life Newman had fought for the place of religion in education, so that in a certain sense he had a congenial theme, and one he had already developed in his *Tamworth Reading Room* letters. In fact, after he left Oxford, secularist and utilitarian ideas spread rapidly in the English universities. He was able to make use of his Oxford experience and hoped to adapt all that he approved of in the system there—and it was much—to the different conditions of Dublin. But whereas at Oxford the dangerous tendency had been in the direction of allowing too little scope to or reducing the influence of Revealed Religion, in the proposed Catholic University the opposite danger was to be feared. Also Newman had to win over the many Catholics who saw no great harm in 'mixed' colleges, and were suspicious of clerically controlled education. He made the basis of his *Discourses* as broad as possible, emphasising that he claimed a place for theology in education on general grounds, without introducing pleadings that applied to any particular religion. He argued that a University is meant to cover a wide circle of knowledge, and so must not exclude theology, and that if it were left aside, other subjects would not be seen in perspective.

I say then, if the various branches of knowledge, which are the matter of teaching in a University, so hang together, that none can be neglected without prejudice to the perfection of the rest, and if Theology be a branch of knowledge, of wide reception, of philosophical structure, of unutterable importance, and of supreme influence, to what conclusion are we brought from these two premisses but this? that to withdraw Theology from the public schools is to impair the completeness and to invalidate the trustworthiness of all that is actually taught in them.

And Newman added:

But I have been insisting simply on Natural Theology, and that, because I wished to carry along with me those who were not Catholics, and, again, as being confident, that no one can really set himself to master and to teach the doctrine of an intelligent Creator in its fullness, without going a great deal further than he at present dreams.

That was the conclusion of the third discourse, and the fourth was summarised as follows:

I have urged that, supposing Theology be not taught, its province will not simply be neglected, but will be actually usurped by other sciences, which will teach, without warrant, conclusions of their own in a subject-matter which needs its own proper principles for its due formation and disposition.[1]

In the remaining lectures Newman, who was writing to two briefs at once and carefully keeping them separate, dealt with the purpose of university education, 'enlargement of mind'. This was

1. *Idea*, pp. 69 and 98

something valuable in itself, the development of our faculties, 'liberal knowledge'. The fifth discourse, 'knowledge its own end', concludes:

> To open the mind, to correct it, to refine it, to enable it to know, and to digest, master, rule, and use its knowledge, to give it power over its own faculties, application, flexibility, method, critical exactness, sagacity, resource, address, eloquent expression, is an object as intelligible (for here we are inquiring, not what the object of a Liberal Education is worth, nor what use the Church makes of it, but what it is in itself), I say, an object as intelligible as the cultivation of virtue, while, at the same time it is absolutely distinct from it.

Earlier in the *Discourse* Newman distinguished clearly the natural, earthly purpose of a university, and explained:

> Liberal Education makes not the Christian, not the Catholic, but the gentleman. It is well to be a gentleman, it is well to have a cultivated intellect, a delicate taste, a candid, equitable, dispassionate mind, a noble and courteous bearing in the conduct of life;—these are the connatural qualities of a large knowledge; they are the objects of a University.

These qualities are not virtue, though they sometimes look like it.

> Quarry the granite rock with razors, or moor the vessel with a thread of silk; then may you hope with such keen and delicate instruments as human knowledge and human reason to contend against those giants, the passion and pride of man.[1]

The danger was that the new university would turn out to be a religious seminary, so that it was very important to emphasise its autonomy and its real purpose. This purpose was not altered because it was Catholic, any more than that of a hospital if it happened to be run by nuns. Hence the famous definition of a gentleman—'he is one who never inflicts pain'—at the end of the eighth discourse, portrays the ideal product of a university, prescinding altogether from religion.

> Such are some of the lineaments of the ethical character, which the cultivated intellect will form, apart from religious principle. They are seen within the pale of the Church and without it, in holy men and in profligate . . .[2]

1. *Idea*, pp. 120–3 2. *Idea*, pp. 208–11

In the final *Discourse*, 'Duties of the Church towards Knowledge', Newman discusses the ways in which Physical Science and Literature may tend to conflict with Revealed Religion. As to the former 'Nature and Grace, Reason and Revelation, come from the same Divine Author, whose works cannot contradict each other', and as to the latter, 'from the nature of the case, if Literature is to be made a study of human nature, you cannot have a Christian Literature. It is a contradiction in terms to attempt a sinless Literature of sinful men.'[1] This last point had to be insisted on. Newman was about to found a University for laymen, not a Seminary, and there were too many (such as the Abbé Gaume, the proscriber of the pagan classics) whose idea of education was to keep Catholics in a state of permanent tutelage, away from all that was 'dangerous'. 'For why do we educate,' Newman asks, 'except to prepare for the World?' and he argues:

If then a University is a direct preparation for this world, let it be what it professes. It is not a Convent, it is not a Seminary; it is a place to fit men of the world for the world. We cannot possibly prevent them plunging into the world, with all its ways and principles and maxims when their time comes; but we can prepare them against what is inevitable; and it is not the way to learn to swim in troubled waters, never to have gone into them . . . cut out from your class books all broad manifestations of the natural man; and those manifestations are waiting for your pupil's benefit at the very doors of your lecture room in living and breathing substance. They will meet him there in all the charm of novelty, and all the fascination of genius or of amiableness. . . . You have refused him the masters of human thought, who would in some sense have educated him, because of their incidental corruption: you have shut up from him those whose thoughts strike home in our hearts, whose words are proverbs, whose names are indigenous to all the world, who are the standard of their mother tongue, and the pride and boast of their countrymen, Homer, Ariosto, Cervantes, Shakespeare, because the old Adam smelt rank in them; and for what have you reserved him? You have given him 'a liberty unto' the multitudinous blasphemy of his day; you have made him free of its newspapers, its reviews, its magazines, its novels, its controversial pamphlets. . . . You have succeeded but in this,—in making the world his University.[2]

Newman opened the University on 3 November 1854, with a first-rate staff of professors and a handful of students. This opening had been delayed by the divisions among the Irish

1. *Idea*, pp. 219–29 2. *Idea*, pp. 232–3

bishops, which were to be a permanent hindrance to success. In practice Archbishop Cullen in Dublin was the effective controller of the University, and a number of the bishops, who were opposed to him on political grounds entirely independent of the University, were lukewarm towards it in consequence. Cullen on the other hand, was distrustful of Newman, and began by thwarting in Rome, early in 1854, his appointment as a bishop, after this had been publicly announced. The status of bishop would have given him just the standing he needed in face of the Irish hierarchy. However, Cullen's distrust increased immeasurably when he found that Newman was making friends with and appointing as professors a number of brilliant 'Young Irelanders'. These Nationalists were in Cullen's eyes no better than the Italian revolutionaries, yet he objected when Newman appointed, chiefly as Professors of Classics, a few of the most distinguished of the English converts. Nonetheless, Newman, thanks to much practical and detailed exertion, built up the University. The whole idea and scheme was worked out as a unity, no point neglected, every opening followed up. Inaugural lectures made the University known, essays were written to explain it historically, statutes carefully drafted and a constitution set going, a flourishing Medical School established, and a Science Faculty with provision for research. The University had its own natural end, and for the moral and religious welfare of the students there were the University church, which Newman built, and the Halls of Residence. These had their tutors, but there was no longer the need there had been at Oxford to stress the 'pastoral' side of their office. In a Catholic University many things could be taken for granted. Indeed just as Newman's sermons as a Catholic give an impression of relaxation and blossoming after the austere simplicity of those at St. Mary's, so his way of conducting a university appears broader and more humanist at Dublin than at Oriel. In laying down the rules of discipline at Dublin he wrote:

> I shall begin by laying down as a guiding principle, what I believe to be the truth, that the young for the most part cannot be driven, but, on the other hand, are open to persuasion and the influence of kindness and personal attachment; and that, in consequence, they are to be kept straight by indirect contrivances rather than by authoritative enactments and naked prohibitions.[1]

1. *My Campaign in Ireland*, 1896, p. 115

Newman arranged a debating society for the students (to which he had objected at Oxford), had a billiard-room built, a cricket-field provided, and did not object to undergraduates who could afford it hunting in top-boots and pink coats.

The University was for the laity and Newman wanted them to gain control of it, but the Irish gentry were 'both suspicious and hopeless of episcopal enterprises', which, of course, the University was, and left it to be supported largely by collections from the poor in the churches. Newman sought the names of as many prominent laymen as he could, in addition to those of bishops and priests, as associates of the University. He wanted eventually to give these associates a real share in its government. He fought for a lay committee to superintend the finances, but this was never allowed. He made a point of having laymen as professors except in such subjects as theology, and of his thirty-two professors, only five were priests. He found himself increasingly thwarted by what he called the 'impracticability' of Archbishop Cullen, who left his pressing requests and letters unanswered for months, and then made decisions without informing the Rector of the University. The dream that Englishmen and Americans would frequent it was never realised. When Newman grasped that it was to be a purely Irish affair, and still more when he found that his presence in his own Oratory, where his first duty lay, was urgently required, he returned to Birmingham, resigning his Rectorship in November 1858, seven years after he had accepted it. He went on working for the University until the end, trying to set up new Halls of Residence, establishing the *Atlantis*, a learned periodical which brought the University much prestige, and opening successful evening-classes for the Dublin young men, fifteen years before university extension lectures were begun elsewhere. These had an attendance of over a hundred, but in the University itself there were barely as many students, distributed in the four faculties of Theology, Philosophy and Letters, Science, and Medicine. The University suffered from the handicap of being unable to grant degrees. Various attempts were made to obtain a charter from the Government, but they broke down before the refusal of the Irish bishops to allow the University to be autonomous. Nevertheless it survived until 1882, when what was left of it was associated with the Royal University of Ireland.

In spite of what is sometimes said or thought to the contrary,

Newman was held in the highest esteem in Ireland, and himself thoroughly appreciated the qualities of the Irish. In October 1858, John O'Hagan, the Professor of Political Economy, after hearing how Cullen had been behaving, wrote:

I fear your associations in connexion with Ireland will dwell very unfavourably in your memory, as a country that never understood or appreciated you. Well,—so far as regards the Irish Professors in the University, (I speak of those whom I know as laymen), it is quite the opposite. We have felt that you only wanted power and freedom of action to make the institution march.

In his reply, Newman said: 'I have experienced nothing but kindness and attention, of which I am quite unworthy, from every class of person in Ireland, whom I have come near.' The only exceptions were Archbishop Cullen, and Archbishop MacHale, who was opposed to Cullen, and in consequence acted rudely to Newman. 'To all the other Bishops I feel exceedingly grateful—If I don't use the word "grateful" about the Professors, it is because I should use much warmer and more intimate terms in speaking of them.' One of them, John Hungerford Pollen, the Professor of Fine Arts, in his reminiscences of Newman in Dublin wrote: 'He shed cheerfulness as a sunbeam sheds light, even while many difficulties were pressing. . . . What a time it was! . . . walking with him in times of recreation . . . listening to talk that was never didactic and never dull.'[1] The year after he left Ireland Newman described, in 'The Northmen and Normans in England and Ireland', the impression of the English Catholic visitor:

He penetrates into the heart of the country; and he recognises an innocence in the young face, and a piety and patience in the aged voice, which strikingly and sadly contrast with the habits of his own rural population. . . . He finds the population as munificent as it is pious, and doing greater works for God out of their poverty, than the rich and noble elsewhere accomplish in their abundance. He finds them characterised by a love of kindred so tender and faithful, as to lead them, on their compulsory expatriation, to send back from their first earnings in another hemisphere incredible sums, with the purpose of bringing over to it those dear ones whom they have left in the old country. And he finds himself received with that warmth of hospitality which has ever been Ireland's boast; and as far as he is personally concerned, his blood is forgotten in his baptism.[2]

1. Anne Pollen, *John Hungerford Pollen*, London 1912, pp. 263–4
2. *Historical Sketches*, III, pp. 257–8

CHAPTER 7

The Defence of the Laity: the *Apologia* (1859-64)

WRITING to John Hungerford Pollen early in 1859, Newman spoke of 'that unruffled faith in the Catholic Church' which they both possessed, but also of their 'common conviction of the miserable deficiencies that exist'. These were present in what Newman never for a moment doubted to be 'the one true fold of the Redeemer'. It was the guardian of Revealed Religion, and had the divine promise that it could not fail in any essential way. Yet within this Catholic Church revealed truths could be obscured or exaggerated, the great Christian privileges and the Divine Indwelling could be insufficiently appreciated. The position of bishops and still more that of the laity could be underestimated, that of the ever more centralised papacy, clinging to its temporal power, overemphasised. In his second novel, *Callista*, written in 1855, Newman described a decayed Christian community in North Africa in the third century, and there was thought to be an implied criticism. He took immense pains over the historical background. In the heroine, the pagan image painter, Callista, he brings out vividly his idea of the Christian Church, and of the genesis of faith. The holy priest Caecilius (St Cyprian) explains to her about our Lord:

> The nearer we draw to Him, the more triumphantly does he enter into us; the longer He dwells in us, the more intimately have we possession of Him. It is an espousal for eternity. This is why it is so easy for us to die for our faith, at which the world marvels.

Callista turns over in her mind this and what two other Christians, a female slave and a country youth, had told her:

> Now the three witnesses who had addressed her about Christianity had each of them made it to consist in the intimate Divine Presence in the

heart. It was the friendship or mutual love of person with person. Here was the very teaching which already was so urgently demanded both by her reason and her heart, which she found nowhere else.[1]

However, Newman did not feel called upon to remedy doctrinal deficiencies in Catholicism. As he said, in 1857, in the preface to *Sermons Preached on Various Occasions*, after 'embracing the Catholic Religion, it was, if not his intention, at least his expectation, that he should never write again on any doctrinal subject'. He thought of discussing questions of philosophy or church history or controversy or literature, 'but it seemed to him incongruous that one, who had so freely taught and published error in a Protestant communion, should put himself forward as a dogmatic teacher in the Catholic Church'.[2] His volume of sermons, most of them preached in the University Church in Dublin, and resembling once more those from the pulpit of St Mary's, was definitely an exception. He had spent his early years as a Catholic founding first the English Oratory and then the Irish University at the request of the Pope. Now he would try to remedy some of the 'miserable deficiencies' on the practical and apologetic level which were hindering the cause of the Church in her preaching of Revealed Religion in England.

One of these was the poor standard of Catholic education, which made it difficult for Catholics to pull their weight or exert their proper influence in the English world. To remedy this, Newman founded, in May 1859, the Oratory School, which, while training Catholic boys religiously, was intended to give them as good an education as that to be had in the public schools. They were to be trusted and to learn responsibility. It was hoped at first, with unreal optimism, that they would go to the University at Dublin, which had been handicapped by the inadequate schooling of many of its students. Newman's Oratory School, while remaining small, proved a real success, and its example and competition raised the standard of the other Catholic schools.

Another crying need was the renewal of the intellectual defence of Revealed Religion. In 1857 Newman began working on a philosophical treatise in defence of Christianity, labelling his first notes *Opus Magnum*. It was held up by the request of the English bishops that he should translate the Bible, to which he

1. *Callista*, pp. 222 and 293
2. *Sermons Preached on Various Occasions*, p. v

gave much time, but which they abandoned at the first difficulty. It was then hindered by the affair of the *Rambler* and the laity. Newman became involved in this both by his interest in the laity and by that in a critical and scholarly periodical, which in England was the only upholder of the Catholic cause in the intellectual sphere.

The *Rambler* was founded in 1848 as a literary magazine for educated Catholics, and as one that would present the Catholic case among educated people generally. In 1858 Sir John Acton, Döllinger's brilliant pupil, and Richard Simpson, a married convert clergyman, became its proprietors, the latter having already acted as sub-editor for two years. For a decade it had set a standard never surpassed since among English Catholics, but it had begun to arouse the ire of Cardinal Wiseman and the bishops. This was partly for personal reasons and partly on account of theological criticisms, especially those of Simpson, who enjoyed pointing out Catholic shortcomings. A crisis was reached early in 1859, which involved the very question of the province of the laity. The Government had just appointed a Royal Commission on elementary education, but without a Catholic representative, the Catholic Poor Schools Committee having put in its claim to one too late. Although the Catholic schools received Government grants, the bishops decided not to co-operate with the Commission, chiefly because it would enquire (among other things) into the methods of religious teaching.

In the *Rambler* for January there appeared an article on the Royal Commission by Scott Nasmyth Stokes, since 1853 one of the Catholic Inspectors of Schools appointed by the Government. He was the leading Catholic lay authority on the school question, and he felt it his duty to give his considered opinion, based on practical experience, and with due submission to ecclesiastical authority, on a matter which concerned so many of the laity. He disputed the grounds on which co-operation with the Royal Commission had been refused and urged that a policy of isolation was suicidal. State-supported schools would simply take the place of denominational ones. Stokes' article was violently attacked in the *Tablet* as being disloyal to the bishops. Stokes replied calmly in the February *Rambler* that blame lay rather with the Poor Schools Committee than with the bishops. He maintained, however, that no religious principle was involved, and that the question had been neither thoroughly discussed nor properly understood (presumably by the bishops), adding that he would be surprised if the bishops were 'displeased by the loyal expression of opinions entertained by many Catholics, and supported by arguments that cannot be met'.

Although dismay had been caused among the laity generally by the decision of the bishops, several of these latter now met in London and decided that unless Simpson retired from the *Rambler* and its spirit was changed, they would have to censure it in their pastoral letters. In order to avoid the scandal of a public censure, the bishops begged Newman to intervene with Simpson and persuade him to resign. This Newman succeeded in doing, and there was no direct censure of the *Rambler* in the pastorals. The difficulty, however, was to find another editor acceptable both to the proprietors of the *Rambler* and to the bishops. Only one man fulfilled the requirements, and so Newman himself, after much prayer, and at the wish of his bishop, Ullathorne, and of Cardinal Wiseman, accepted the editorship. His aim was to serve the educated and thinking laity, and preserve an organ which was so valuable for them, while at the same time helping the bishops in a difficulty, and keeping the peace among Catholics. He objected to the tone, not to the principles, of the *Rambler*, and would not disown his friend, Simpson, who was a very generous and devout as well as intelligent Catholic. Thus Newman's announcement at the beginning of the May number, the first for which he was responsible, ran:

In commencing a new series of the *Rambler*, its conductors think it right to state, that they profess no other object in their labours but that which has been the animating principle of the Magazine hitherto, viz., to co-operate with Catholic periodicals of higher pretentions in a work of special importance at the present day,—the refinement, enlargement, and elevation of the intellect in the educated classes.

It will be their aim, as it has ever been, to combine devotion to the Church with discrimination and candour in the treatment of her opponents; to reconcile freedom of thought with implicit faith; to discountenance what is untenable and unreal, without forgetting the tenderness due to the weak and the reverence rightly claimed for what is sacred; and to encourage a manly investigation of subjects of public interest under a deep sense of the prerogatives of ecclesiastical authority.

Years afterwards Newman noted:

In the Advertisement not a word was said of any change . . . in the *Rambler*, though my purpose was in fact to change what had in so many ways displeased me. But I had no wish to damage the fair fame of men who I believed were at bottom sincere Catholics, and I thought it unfair, ungenerous, impertinent and cowardly to make on their behalf acts of confession and contrition, and to make a display of change of editorship, and (as if) so virtuous a change.[1]

There still remained the question of the *Rambler* criticism of the bishops' attitude to the Royal Commission. Newman dealt with that by publishing copious extracts from the pastorals in which Wiseman and Ullathorne defended themselves, followed by two remarks of his own. The first was to the effect that it had not been realised that the bishops had reached a formal decision at the time the *Rambler* articles appeared. The second ran as follows:

Acknowledging then most fully the prerogatives of the episcopate, we do unfeignedly believe . . . that their Lordships really desire to know the opinion of the laity on subjects in which the laity are especially concerned. If even in the preparation of a dogmatic definition the faithful are consulted, as lately in the instance of the Immaculate Conception, it is at least as natural to anticipate such an act of kind feeling and sympathy in great practical questions, out of the condescension which belongs to those who are *forma facti gregis ex animo*. If our words or tone were disrespectful, we deeply grieve and apologise for such a fault; but surely we are not disrespectful in thinking, and in having thought, that the Bishops would like to know the sentiments of an influential portion of the laity before they took any step which perhaps they could not recall. Surely it was no disrespect towards them to desire that they should have the laity rallying round them on the great question of education. . . . We are too fully convinced of the misery of any division between the rulers of the Church and the educated laity . . . to commit ourselves consciously to any act which may tend to so dire a calamity. . . . Let the Bishops pardon, then, the incidental hastiness of manner or want of ceremony of the rude Jack-tars of their vessel, as far as it occurred, in consideration of the zeal and energy with which they haul-to the ropes and man the yards.

Newman soon began to suffer for his chivalrous act. The Ushaw theologian Dr Gillow wrote to him that it was heresy to say the laity were consulted in doctrinal matters. Newman was

1. *Ward*, I, p. 494

able to defend himself and pacify Dr Gillow, but he sent the latter's letter to Bishop Ullathorne, and asked for a theological censor for the *Rambler*. Ullathorne would not commit himself in writing, but called at the Oratory on 22 May. Newman has preserved a minute of the meeting.

The Bishop, who called today, began by saying that he could not undertake the revision of the *Rambler* . . . He thought there were remains of the old spirit. It was irritating. Our laity were a *peaceable* set; the Church was *peace*. They had a deep faith; they did not like to hear that any one doubted . . . I said in answer, that he saw one side, I another; that the Bishops etc did not see that state of the Laity, e.g. in Ireland, how unsettled, yet how docile. He said something like 'who are the laity,' I answered (not those *words*) that the Church would look foolish without them.

Newman tried to convince Ullathorne that he had undertaken the Irish University in 'the hope of doing something towards those various objects for which I had consented to undertake the *Rambler*'. Ullathorne could not see that Newman held a responsible and educated laity to be something essential for the Church. He then expressed the wish that Newman should give up the *Rambler* editorship—this within a month of the appearance of his first number. Newman, of course, promised to do so, and wrote to a friend:

There was no sort of unpleasantness in our conversation from beginning to end. It is impossible with the principles and feelings on which I have acted all through my life that I could have acted otherwise. I never have resisted nor can resist the voice of a lawful Superior speaking in his own province.

Thus Newman's great experiment was stopped before it had fairly begun. His own explanation he gave in a memorandum, three years later, as follows:

It is rather strange the Bishop let me off my engagement so easily, or rather pressed a release on me, when I had gained his side of the bargain, and had not paid my own. Though I had rescued Simpson etc from the Pastorals, I was allowed, or rather urged to give him back the Magazine. Perhaps it was the Cardinal etc, were seized with a panic lest they had got out of the frying pan into the fire.

Newman had unwillingly taken on the *Rambler*, because he thought that was God's will, and now for the same reason he relinquished it. To his friend Henry Wilberforce he wrote:

If you attempt at a wrong time. what in itself is right you perhaps become a heretic or schismatic. . . . When I am gone, it will be seen perhaps that persons stopped me from doing a *work* which I *might* have done. God over-rules all things—Of course it is discouraging to be out of joint with the time, and to be snubbed and stopped as soon as I begin to act.[1]

Newman's troubles were not over. He still had to bring out the July number of the *Rambler*. He determined that he must defend the doctrine he held about the place of the laity in the Church, which he had stated in May, and to which such objection had been taken. Many were in dismay at his resignation, and the doctrine seemed to him an essential part of Revelation on the nature of the Church. This was the origin of the famous article *On Consulting the Faithful in Matters of Doctrine*. In it he showed how an examination of the beliefs of the ordinary faithful was one of the ways of discovering what the truths were that had been revealed: 'the tradition of the Apostles, committed to the whole Church . . . manifests itself variously at various times: sometimes by the mouth of the episcopacy, sometimes by the doctors, sometimes by the people'. None of these channels of tradition was to be neglected and Newman laid great stress on the *Consent of the faithful*. This was something he learned when he studied the Fathers, thirty years before; it underlay the theory of development, the unfolding of what was implicitly held; and Newman had described it towards the end of his *Lectures on the Turks*, in 1853. 'By what channels,' he asked, 'had the divine philosophy descended down from the Great Teacher through three centuries of persecution?' And he replied:

In that earliest age, it was simply the living spirit of the myriads of the faithful, none of them known to fame, who received from the disciples of our Lord, and husbanded so well, and circulated so widely, and transmitted so faithfully, generation after generation, the once delivered apostolic faith; who held it with such sharpness of outline and explicitness of detail, as enabled even the unlearned instinctively to discriminate between truth and error, spontaneously to reject the very shadow of heresy and to be proof against the most brilliant intellects, when they would lead them out of the narrow way.[2]

Now, in the *Rambler* article Newman showed how the Consent of the faithful was more than a witness to the truth. The faithful

1. *Ward*, I, pp. 496–9 2. *Historical Sketches*, I, pp. 209–10

understood the content of the faith instinctively, enlightened in this sphere (as he was to show in *A Grammar of Assent* that they were in ordinary life), by an 'illative sense'. Then, too, they had received and were guided by the Holy Spirit. Lastly, they had a jealousy of error, which they felt at once as a scandal. To illustrate this last point Newman returned to the history which he had discussed in his first book, *The Arians of the Fourth Century*. He showed once more how this was the period when 'the divine tradition committed to the infallible Church was proclaimed and maintained far more by the faithful than by the Episcopate . . .' when 'the divine dogma of our Lord's divinity was proclaimed, enforced, maintained, and (humanly speaking) preserved far more by the "Ecclesia docta" than by the "Ecclesia docens" ', and when 'the body of the episcopate was unfaithful to its commission, while the body of the laity was faithful to its baptism'. He then gave a long array of testimonies to the fidelity of the laity, and to what he called a temporary suspense of the functions of the *Ecclesia docens*, when 'the body of the bishops failed in their confession of the faith', and 'the comparatively few who remained faithful were discredited and driven into exile'. Newman concluded by saying that the teaching Church is more happy when she is surrounded by enthusiastic partisans who appreciate their faith, 'than when she cuts off the faithful from the study of her divine doctrines and the sympathy of her divine contemplations, and requires of them a *fides implicita* in her word, which in the educated classes will terminate in indifference, and in the poorer in superstition'.[1]

Thus was the dispute with the bishops about education lifted to a higher plane. The Church was a Communion, with a common conscience, that of all its members, and was not to be looked on as a mere juridical entity, ruled by officers. Bishops, priests and laity formed one body, and there must be consultation and trust, for the laity were an essential part of the Church. This teaching, which was to be incorporated in the Conciliar Decree on the Church at the Second Vatican Council, was resented among the English Catholic authorities and theologians, but no-one was in a position to dispute Newman's facts. Dr Gillow returned to the attack and wrote to Bishop Brown of Newport, who delated

1. *On Consulting the Faithful in Matters of Doctrine*, edited by John Coulson, London 1961, pp. 75–7, 106

Newman's article to the Congregation of Propaganda in Rome, for heresy. At Propaganda they were shocked, but this was partly because Newman's words had been *mis*translated into Latin for them by Bishop Brown. When Newman heard what had happened, he wrote at once to Cardinal Wiseman, who was in Rome at the time, undertaking to accept whatever dogmas he was supposed to have infringed, and to show that what he had written was absolutely consistent with them. At Propaganda they received Newman's letter and at once made out a list of statements of his to which they objected. This list Wiseman, for reasons unknown, never gave to Newman. Instead he received a letter from Manning to say that Wiseman on his return to England hoped to bring the affair to an end in a way that would be acceptable to Newman. That was the last he heard, and he presumed the matter had been dropped.

At Rome it was thought that Newman was unwilling to reply and a bad impression was created. Mgr Talbot, the convert papal chamberlain, wrote seven years later in a famous letter to Manning (then Archbishop of Westminster): 'It is perfectly *true* that a cloud has been hanging over Dr Newman in Rome ever since the Bishop of Newport delated him to Rome for heresy in his article in the *Rambler*.' The laity were 'beginning to show the cloven hoof', 'putting into practice the doctrine taught by Dr Newman in his article in the *Rambler*'. 'What is the province of the laity? To hunt, to shoot, to entertain. These matters they understand, but to meddle with ecclesiastical matters they have no right at all.' 'Dr Newman is the most dangerous man in England.' Manning's reply to this letter and other letters of his to the same correspondent are very difficult to reconcile with his claim to be Newman's friend. It was this double action of Manning which eventually made Newman tell him plainly, 'I do not know whether I am on my head or my heels when I have active relations with you'.[1] Manning's distrust and opposition to Newman perhaps dates from the period of his *Rambler* article. Manning himself dated it from the end of 1861, when he thought an attack on his views in favour of the Pope's temporal power was in

1. See the verdict of H. I. D. Ryder in *Essays*, London 1911, pp. 280 *et seq.*, 'Manning's Infidelity to the Claims of Friendship in the Case of J. H. Newman'. Ryder was one of Newman's Oratorians, and also Manning's nephew, his mother and Mrs Manning being sisters.

some way approved of by Newman, who in fact knew nothing about it.

The cloud spoken of by Talbot was lifted, in 1867, after eight years, when Ambrose St John and another of Newman's Oratorians went to Rome, and found him blamed there for not having explained the listed passages in his *Rambler* article. Pius IX appealed to Cullen as to Newman's orthodoxy. However much their ideas of a university may have conflicted, Cullen understood Newman better than some of the English converts, and his report was entirely favourable.

During the intervening years, with a suspicion of heresy hanging over him, Newman's influence was undermined, as he noted himself.

> The cause of my not writing from 1859 to 1864 was my failure with the *Rambler*. I thought I had got into a scrape, and it became me to be silent. So they thought at Rome if Mgr Talbot is to be their spokesman . . .[1]

The frustrations in Dublin and over translation of Scripture had not improved his position, but what, with the *Rambler* episode, chiefly undermined his influence was the breach with the London Oratory and its consequences. Newman always recognised that the London Oratory was 'the instrument of much good', but London was the centre to which all the world came, and from the London Oratory went out talk about Newman, which prejudiced an influential part of the Catholic body against him.

Newman suffered, too, for his views about the temporal power of the Pope. During the sad eighteen-sixties Pius IX was clinging to what remained of it, and demanding the support of all the Catholic bishops. Manning even appeared to want it made a dogma. All this seems absurd nowadays, but it was extremely trying to have to hold aloof, as Newman did, when he made it clear that he regarded the temporal power as something quite separate from the spiritual position of the papacy.

These years until 1864, and even later, were for him a real purifying 'dark night'. At one moment it even looked as though the Oratory School would fail, when it went through a crisis of authority and several of the chief masters left. That storm was weathered, but for an active practical man like Newman no trial

1. *A.W.*, p. 272

could be harder than to be kept in idleness, thanks to the undermining of his influence. His devotion to the Church had led him to become a Catholic, and now, after barely fourteen years, he was hindered from working for it. That was his great cross. All through he had been obedient. He stopped the *Tracts for the Times* at a word from his Anglican bishop. He resigned the *Rambler* at Ullathorne's wish. As we shall see, he twice dropped the plan of founding an Oratory at Oxford, to which he had been invited by his bishop, at the request of higher authority. Long ago Abbot Butler vindicated him from the further charge of being oversensitive:

> When count is taken of the nature of the persistent campaign carried on against him in England and in Rome by Ward, Talbot, Coffin, Herbert Vaughan, and with Manning's assent; how such charges as unorthodoxy, unsoundness, disloyalty, worldliness, lowness of view, evil influence, Gallicanism were freely levelled against him during a period of ten years and more; and further when it is remembered that he knew quite well all the time, all that was being spoken and whispered against him . . . not to mind, he must needs have been not merely uncommonly thick-skinned, but even rhinoceros hided.[1]

Newman knew, and in view of the history of the Oxford Movement, he could not help knowing, that God had given him the greatest natural talents, and yet now as a Catholic he found himself condemned to uselessness, his sword rusting in its scabbard, through no fault of his. The very pages in his private journal where he describes his cross enable us also to glimpse the heroic abandonment it occasioned. Through his complaints, the underlying serenity can be felt. As he had remarked long before in one of his Parochial Sermons:

> The foundations of the ocean, the vast realms of water which girdle the earth, are as tranquil and silent in the storm as in a calm. So it is with the souls of holy men. They have a well of peace springing up within them unfathomable, and though the accidents of the hour may make them seem agitated, yet in their hearts they are not so.[2]

Even those who ought to have understood his position were inclined to criticise. During the early sixties, Newman kept silent on the subject of the temporal power, and allowed his

1. Cuthbert Butler, *The Life and Times of Bishop Ullathorne*, London 1926, II, p. 312
2. *P.S.*, V, p. 69

opinions to be inferred (as indeed they were at once by his opponents). Some who shared his views complained that he did not speak out, although he had no special call to do so, and would have damaged his Oratory and his school fruitlessly. His prudence preserved these and the causes he stood for until better times. Acton and Simpson were now carrying on the *Rambler*, and continued to drag into important articles digressions and asides that hit at the Church authorities. Newman wished they, too, would use prudence and tact. His wise advice has recently been used as the ground for an accusation that he was willing 'to subordinate historical truth to ecclesiastical expediency'. His whole life refutes the charge. Those minute patristic studies into historical truth were one of the original sources of his power, and they had led him to make the greatest sacrifices. Facts were sacred; theories of development or of theology must always give way before them. At the end of 1859, in a *Rambler* article on St John Chrysostom, he spoke of 'the endemic perennial fidget which possesses us about giving scandal; facts are omitted in great histories, or glosses are put upon memorable acts, because they are thought not edifying, whereas of all scandals such omissions, such glosses, are the greatest'. A little later his excuse for not writing books was that in the atmosphere of those days, 'unless one doctored all one's facts, one would be thought a bad Catholic'.[1] Newman had not only tact and obedience but also that important quality *le sens du possible*, which Acton lacked. With it Acton could have tided the *Rambler* over the difficult years after Newman's editorship, and enabled it to continue the valuable work of educating Catholics in critical and adult standards. In fact, the *Rambler* and the *Home and Foreign Review* that succeeded it, had to be abandoned, and during the key years before the First Vatican Council, the moderate English Catholics were left without a means of stating their case, and of defending themselves against the extreme ultramontanes.

Newman's views on the relation of history and dogma were, like all his views, guided by his belief in Revealed Religion. In his lecture on 'Christianity and Scientific Investigation', delivered in 1855 and now forming part of *The Idea of a University*, he lays down of the true representative of the 'imperial intellect' that, 'If he has one cardinal maxim in his philosophy, it is, that

1. *Historical Sketches*, II, p. 231; *Ward*, I, p. 572

truth cannot contradict truth; if he has a second, it is, that truth often *seems* to contradict truth; and, if a third, it is the practical conclusion that we must be patient with such appearances, and not be hasty to pronounce them to be really of a more formidable character'. Later in the lecture Newman says, 'while this free discussion is, to say the least, so safe for Religion, or rather so expedient, it is on the other hand simply necessary for progress in Science'.[1] He was soon to have the opportunity of delving further into the whole question.

At the beginning of 1864 Newman appeared to be a neglected, powerless man. There were only six others besides himself at his Oratory in Birmingham; he was forgotten by most Protestants, misunderstood by many Catholics, and distrusted by their chief authorities. Then, suddenly and unexpectedly power was restored to him as he entered upon his sixty-fourth year. Charles Kingsley, in a review of his brother-in-law, James Anthony Froude's *History of England* for the January number of *Macmillan's Magazine*, gratuitously introduced Newman's name.

Truth for its own sake, had never been a virtue with the Roman clergy. Father Newman informs us that it need not, and on the whole ought not to be; that cunning is the weapon which heaven has given to the Saints wherewith to withstand the brute male force of the wicked world which marries and is given in marriage. Whether his notion be doctrinally correct or not, it is at least historically so.

Kingsley was already a well-known novelist, besides being Professor of Modern History at Cambridge and tutor to the Prince of Wales. The correspondence which followed Newman summarised in a famous piece of irony.

Mr Kingsley begins by exclaiming,—'O the chicanery, the wholesale fraud, the vile hypocrisy, the conscience-killing tyranny of Rome! We have not far to seek for an evidence of it. There's Father Newman to wit: one living specimen is worth a hundred dead ones. He, a Priest writing of Priests, tells us that lying is never any harm.'

I interpose: 'You are taking a most extraordinary liberty with my name. If I have said this, tell me when and where.'

Mr Kingsley replies: 'You said it, Reverend Sir, in a Sermon which you preached, when a Protestant, as Vicar of St Mary's, and published in 1844; and I could read you a very salutary lecture on the effects which that Sermon had at the time on my own opinion of you.'

1. *Idea*, pp. 461 and 471

I make answer: 'Oh . . . *Not*, it seems, as a Priest speaking of Priests;—but let us have the passage.'

Mr Kingsley relaxes: 'Do you know, I like your *tone*. From your *tone* I rejoice, greatly rejoice, to be able to believe that you did not mean what you said.'

I rejoin: '*Mean* it! I maintain I never *said* it, whether as a Protestant or as a Catholic.'

Mr Kingsley replies: 'I waive that point.'

I object: 'Is it possible! What? waive the main question! I either said it or I didn't. You have made a monstrous charge against me, direct, distinct, public. You are bound to prove it as directly, as distinctly, as publicly;—or to own you can't.'

'Well,' says Mr. Kingsley, 'if you are quite sure you did not say it, I'll take your word for it; I really will.'

My *word*! I am dumb. Somehow I thought that it was my *word* that happened to be on trial. . . .[1]

Kingsley retorted in a long pamphlet, *What then does Dr. Newman Mean*? Newman decided that there was only one charge against him, that of untruthfulness, and it was accepted by many in England who thought he had led a secret Catholic movement to undermine the Church of England, while still a member of it. This imputation had lain on him for twenty years, and now he had the opportunity to remove it. 'I am bound now as a duty to myself, to the Catholic cause, to the Catholic Priesthood, to give an account of myself without any delay, when I am so rudely and circumstantially charged with untruthfulness. . . .' 'I must, I said, give the true key to my whole life; I must show what I am that it may be seen what I am not, and that the phantom may be extinguished which gibbers instead of me. . . . I will vanquish, not my Accuser, but my judges,' that is, the English people.[2] The result was the *Apologia*, which appeared in weekly parts from April to June 1864. Now that it is known as one of the world's famous books, it is difficult to realise that Newman's victory was by no means assured. Not merely was England still strongly Protestant, but the prejudice against him as a secret traitor was widespread. However, what struck home was the frankness of his account of his progress from the Church of

1. Newman omitted this passage, when he republished the *Apologia* in 1865, and thus it is not in the uniform edition. Some modern editions have reprinted it.
2. First edition of the *Apologia*, pp. 31 and 47

England to that of Rome. Dean Church reviewing the *Apologia* in the *Guardian* in June 1864, said:

Those who know Dr. Newman's powers and are acquainted with his career, and know to what it led him, and yet persist in the charge of insincerity and dishonesty against one who probably has made the greatest sacrifice of our generation to his convictions of truth, will be able to pick up from his own narrative much that they would not otherwise have known, to confirm and point the old familiar views cherished by dislike and narrowness.

In the *Apologia*, as in all his writing, Newman showed his power of entering into the minds of others and stating their views and arguments even more clearly than they did themselves. Dean Church continued:

Whatever may be thought of many details, the effect and lesson of the whole will not be lost on minds of any generosity, on whatever side they may be: they will be touched with the confiding nobleness which has kept back nothing, which has stated its case with its weak points and its strong, and with full consciousness of what was weak as well as of what was strong, which has surrendered its whole course of conduct, just as it has been, to be scrutinised, canvassed, and judged.[1]

He went on to say that the interest of the *Apologia* was personal rather than controversial. Undoubtedly Newman was vindicating his personal honour and truthfulness in the years preceding his entry into the Roman Church, but he was also defending the Catholic priesthood from Kingsley's violent accusations. This he did in the last few pages of Part VII, the last part of the *Apologia*, 'General Answer to Mr Kingsley', which was later called 'Position of My Mind since 1845'. The earlier pages of this Part VII were devoted to the subject of the infallibility of the Church, or as Newman put it, to answering the charge: 'that I, as a Catholic, not only make profession to hold doctrines which I cannot possibly believe in my heart, but that I also believe in the existence of a power on earth, which at its own will imposes upon men any new set of *credenda*, when it pleases, by a claim to infallibility; in consequence, that my own thoughts are not my own property; that I cannot tell that tomorrow I may not have to give up what I hold to-day, and that the necessary effect of such a condition of mind must be a degrading bondage . . .'[2] This was the supreme

1. R. W. Church, *Occasional Papers*, II, pp. 383–5
2. *Apo.*, p. 246

accusation, which cut at the root of the claim made by the Roman Church to be the champion of Revealed Religion in every age. So far from being its champion, it appeared to subordinate Revelation to the *ipse dixit* of its own infallibility. The topic had become a burning one owing to the condemnation by Pius IX, at the end of January 1864, of the Congress of German Catholic scholars held at Munich under the presidency of Professor Döllinger, in the previous September. Döllinger had stressed the importance of the historical and critical study of theology, and of distinguishing Revelation from mere hypotheses. He deprecated the denunciations and censures which discouraged serious researchers, and spoke slightingly of scholastic theology. He also compared the German theological school with the Roman, the former was fighting with cannons, the latter with bows and arrows. The 'Munich Brief' of Pius IX disapproved of the attacks on scholasticism made at the Congress, and deplored the fact that it had met without a mandate from the hierarchy, whose duty it was to keep watch over theology. It also laid down that the Catholic scholar was bound not only by the solemn definitions of the Church but also by the 'ordinary magisterium', the decisions of the Roman Curial Congregations, and by the common teaching of theologians. Newman analysed the Brief carefully and came to the conclusion that it denied to scientists the 'elbow room' they required for their researches, that 'free discussion' he had maintained in his lectures at Dublin to be 'simply necessary for progress in Science'. In his analysis he wrote:

> Well, I am not likely to investigate in science—but I certainly could not write a word upon the special controversies and difficulties of the day with a view to defend religion from free thinking physicists without allowing them freedom of logic in their own science—so that, if I understand this Brief, it is simply a providential intimation to every religious man, that, at this moment, we are simply to be silent, while scientific investigation proceeds—and say not a word on questions of interpretation of Scripture etc etc, when perplexed persons ask us—and I am not sure that it will not prove to be the best course.[1]

One consequence of the Munich Brief was that Acton brought to an end the *Home and Foreign Review*, the successor of the *Rambler*. He considered its whole attitude to be opposed to that

1. *Ward*, I, p. 642

of the Holy See as represented by the Brief, and the last number appeared in April 1864. On 10 April Acton wrote to Newman saying that if he replied to Kingsley, he should widen the scope of his reply to go into some of the questions in which the *Home and Foreign* had been involved. He also urged that Newman should 'enlighten not only the Protestants but such Catholics as have got a little confused by the policy which is adopted in order to avoid scandal', and should deal with 'the difficulty which many seem to feel in the practice of proscribing truth and positively encouraging falsehood in the Church'. Newman replied, 'As to the points you mention, you may be sure I shall go as far as ever I can'. The result was that first half of Part VII of the *Apologia*, 'Position of my mind since 1845'. There Newman on the one hand defended and showed the limits of the Church's infallibility, and on the other, protested against authoritarianism. He began by confessing his own certainty of the being of God, yet that 'the world seems simply to give the lie to that great truth, of which my whole being is so full'. But if it was the will of God 'to interfere in human affairs, and to make provision for retaining in the world a knowledge of Himself, so definite and distinct as to be proof against the energy of human scepticism', then it would not be surprising 'if He should think fit to introduce a power into the world, invested with the prerogative of infallibility in religious matters'. The Catholic Church claimed to possess this prerogative. Newman, without discussing where in practice the seat of this power lay, professed his whole-hearted submission to it. He then showed its limits. 'The great truths of the moral law, of natural religion, and of Apostolic faith, are both its boundary and its foundation. It must not go beyond them, and it must ever appeal to them. Both its subject-matter, and its articles in that subject-matter, are fixed. And it must ever profess to be guided by Scripture and by tradition. It must refer to the particular Apostolic truth which it is enforcing, or (what is called) *defining*.' Nothing could be presented as part of the Christian faith, which was not in some way included in Revelation. Newman thus replied to the charge that the Church could 'impose upon men any new set of *credenda* when it pleases'.[1]

He then proceeded to the difficulties raised by the Munich Brief. There was a great trial to reason in the Catholic Church's

1. *Apo.*, p. 253

claim to interfere in matters which lay beyond the limits assigned to it by Revelation. In order to preserve Revealed truth, it claimed the power 'to animadvert on opinions in secular matters which bear upon religion, on matters of philosophy, of science, of literature, and of history'. But, 'in all such cases the question of faith does not come in at all'. It is rather a matter of discipline, and although the Church must be obeyed 'perhaps in process of time it will tacitly recede from its own injunctions'. Those who possessed the protection of infallibility were by no means always infallible. Newman admitted, 'I think history supplies us with instances in the Church, where legitimate power has been harshly used', but in this sphere 'We are called upon, not to profess anything, but to submit and be silent'. Yet on the whole, authority had been in the right, and there was a time for everything, whether the reformation of an abuse or the development of a doctrine. On the other hand, it could be very discouraging when authority was 'supported by a violent ultra party, which exalts opinions into dogmas, and has it principally at heart to destroy every school of thought but its own'.[1] Especially trying in that case was the position of those who were attempting to reconcile the wonderful new discoveries of science with Revelation. In view of this and of the inherent difficulty of deciding what exactly was proved by science, Newman concluded that for the present the wise thing was to keep silent, and, referring to the Munich Brief, he added: 'I interpret recent acts of the highest Catholic authority as fulfilling my expectation; I interpret them as tying the hands of a controversialist such as I should be.' Newman went on to ask whether infallible authority had in fact 'destroyed the energy of the Catholic intellect'. He replied that in the case of Galileo the exception proved the rule, and showed how, in previous centuries, the Roman Church had been so very slow to interfere in controversies, and that independence of mind was not in fact destroyed. Controversies raged in a local university, or before a local bishop, and then moved elsewhere. Appeal might be made to inferior authorities, generations would pass, the question be well ventilated, and even then only so vaguely decided that it remained an open question. That way of proceeding gave courage to the individual theologian or controversialist. 'He would not dare to do this, if he knew an authority,

1. *Apo.*, pp. 257–60

which was supreme and final, was watching every word he said, and made signs of assent or dissent to each sentence, as he uttered it. Then indeed he would be fighting, as the Persian soldiers, under the lash.' Newman concluded that the multitude of nations in the Catholic Church was a further protection against narrowness, and, accepting the thesis of Döllinger, said: 'I trust that all European races will ever have a place in the Church, and assuredly I think that the loss of the English, not to say the German element, in its composition has been a most serious misfortune.'[1]

1. *Apo.*, pp. 263–9

CHAPTER 8

Catholic Extremism in Education and in Doctrine (1864-75)

AFTER the appearance of the *Apologia* the power which Newman had lost was suddenly restored to him. English people generally were convinced of his integrity, and once more, whatever he said or wrote, he could be sure of a hearing. Many Anglicans renewed their friendship with him after holding aloof for twenty years. Keble, Church and Rogers actually helped him in the writing of the *Apologia*. Catholics regarded him once more as their champion, and the vindicator of their clergy. The old Catholic priests, who always preferred Newman's moderation to the extremism of many of the converts, rallied to his support, and addresses of congratulation signed by them came in, especially from the populous northern dioceses. The ultramontanes were not pleased. Manning wrote to Talbot in Rome about two of the leading Westminister clergy who were organising an address to Newman: 'Oakeley and Dr Maguire have been literally playing the fool about him in this Kingsley affair.' The only public notice Manning took of the *Apologia* was to criticise, in a pamphlet against Pusey, Newman's remarks on the difficulty of logical proof of God's existence, without mentioning him by name. The young Herbert Vaughan wrote of the book to the wife of William George Ward: 'There are views put forward which I abhor, and which fill me with pain and suspicion.'

As for Newman, he regarded his restored position merely as giving him the opportunity to work. Already in the last part of the *Apologia* he had used his new power to resist the cramping narrowness of the Munich Brief, which made the acceptance of Revealed Religion so unnecessarily difficult. An urgent need was that of higher education for Catholics. The *Apologia* was barely completed when Bishop Ullathorne spontaneously offered Newman the mission, the Catholic parish, at Oxford, which lay in his diocese.

Ullathorne's idea was that Newman should build a church in the town, and also make provision for the religious needs of Catholics at the University. Lay people were mostly in favour of their sons going there and the Bishops had taken no decisive step against it. The English Catholics had never shown the least inclination to send their sons to the Dublin Catholic University, and since 1854, thanks to the abolition of religious tests, Oxford and Cambridge were open to them. According to Newman's ideas, if the laity were to occupy the place that was theirs in the Church, and if they were to enter the main-stream of their country's life, such higher education was essential. Unfortunately Manning, already influential, and who became Archbishop of Westminster after Wiseman's death in 1865, was strongly opposed to Catholics going to Oxford, and even more to Newman's going there. This was on the abstract principle that 'mixed education' was dangerous and bad. Many of the English bishops favoured a more realistic policy, and saw that the wishes of their loyal and patient laity must be taken into account. Manning had the support of a number of the converts, who had also enjoyed the benefits of an Oxford education, which they represented as dangerous, like that of the free-thinking Continental universities, so anathema in Italian eyes. A set of tendentious questions was drawn up and sent to various converts, the answers to be forwarded to the Congregation of Propaganda in Rome. These questions were not sent to Newman, but after being shown a friend's copy of them, he remarked that they might all have been summed up in one, 'Are you or are you not one of those wicked men who advocate Oxford education?' They assumed that the clergy could not go to Oxford and asked, 'Ought the principle to be admitted that the laity should be more highly educated than the clergy?' Left to itself, the Congregation of Propaganda would have done whatever the English bishops advised, but Manning used his influence with Wiseman, and then in Rome with Propaganda, as his letters preserved there confirm, against Catholics going to the English universities. Propaganda now ordered the English bishops to discuss the matter, and a meeting was hurriedly called on 13 December 1864. There it was agreed that Catholics should be discouraged from going to Oxford, but nine out of twelve of the bishops were very doubtful of anything like a complete prohibition. An appeal by laymen to Propaganda was not heeded, and in view of the episcopal conclusion, Newman was obliged to sell the land he had bought for an Oratory. In March 1865 the bishops met, and decided, not on a prohibition, but on a very strong dissuasive.

However, in the summer of 1866, Ullathorne, still anxious for his church, again asked Newman to go to Oxford and offered him the mission there. Newman was convinced that Catholic parents would continue to send their sons to University, but after his previous experiences, would only accept if formal permission were obtained from Propaganda for the foundation of an Oratory. This was forthcoming, but the enemies of Oxford education secured that with it went a secret instruction that Newman himself was not to reside in Oxford, lest he should attract more Catholics there than would otherwise be the case. If he made plans to reside, he was to be dissuaded 'blande suaviterque' (transliterated, blandly and suavely). Ullathorne hoped to get this secret condition removed, but meanwhile Newman collected subscriptions from his friends for the new Oratory, and large sums were given, on the assumption that he would go to Oxford. In March 1867 a letter from the Roman correspondent of the Catholic *Weekly Register* revealed the secret instruction, and gave as the reason for it the suspicions of Newman's orthodoxy. 'Only an ultramontane without a taint in his fidelity could enter such an arena as Oxford. . . .' The laity were indignant and an address signed by almost all the leading laymen of the day was sent to Newman, in which they said, 'we feel that every blow that touches you inflicts a wound upon the Catholic Church in this country'. It was after this that Ambrose St John went to Rome to vindicate Newman there, and discovered how the letter asking him to explain passages in the article 'On Consulting the Laity' had never reached him. Manning was quite determined that Newman should not go to Oxford, and later in the summer the idea of an Oratory there was finally abandoned. Nowadays when Catholics go freely to Oxford and other universities it is difficult to understand the reasons put forward to justify the prohibition. As Newman remarked at the time: '*all places are dangerous,*—the world is dangerous. I do not believe that Oxford is more dangerous than Woolwich, than the army, than London,—and I think you cannot keep young men under glass cases.'[1] In fact Catholics were deprived of proper higher education for thirty years, until after Manning died. The ban on Oxford was removed in 1895, but its

1. *Ward*, II, p. 136

harmful effects on English Catholics naturally lasted much longer. About the religious side of Oxford, Newman had written in 1860:

While I do not see my way to weaken the Church of England, being what it is, least of all should I be disposed to do so in Oxford, which has hitherto been the seat of those traditions which constitute whatever there is of Catholic doctrine and practice in the Anglican Church. Oxford deserves least of any part of Anglican territory to be interfered with. That there are false traditions there I know well . . . but, till things are very much changed there, in weakening Oxford we are weakening our friends, weakening our own de facto παιδαγωγὸς into the Church. Catholics did not make us Catholics; Oxford made us Catholics. . . . In all that I have written, I have spoken of Oxford and the Oxford system with affection and admiration. I have put its system forward as an instance of that union of dogmatic teaching and liberal education, which command my assent.'

To Pusey Newman wrote in 1866: 'I should come to Oxford for the sake of the Catholic youth there, who are likely to be, in the future, more numerous than they are now, and my first object *after* that would be to soften prejudice against Catholicism.'[1]

It was not sufficient to prohibit Catholics from going to the Universities; some alternative had to be provided. It was clear that most Catholics, including the clergy, would have preferred to see the prohibition removed, but Manning was adamant. The only alternative was some kind of Catholic University or College. In 1874 Manning founded one at Kensington, which was a disastrous failure. Already on 9 April 1872 in a letter to the President of Oscott, Newman had rejected the idea of a Catholic University 'for I think our present rulers would never give us a real one'. The laity would not be allowed any genuine control, and intellectual freedom would not be assured. 'I dread a minute and jealous supervision on the part of authority which will hamper every act of the heads of the University,' and 'I surely anticipate the active animosity to whatever is wise in their administration, on the part of an ultra clique, whose gossip is taken at Rome and by Propaganda for nothing short of gospel.' Newman summarised his attitude for the benefit of his friend, Emily Bowles, in a letter of 8 June 1872:

You may say from and for me three things to anyone you please. (1) That I never have by word or act advocated the scheme of a Catholic

1. *Ward*, II, pp. 57, 121

College at Oxford, though many have attributed such a scheme to me. What I alone took part in was the establishment of an Oratory there to protect Catholic youths residing in Protestant Colleges.
(2) And what I advocated then I advocate now. In a hard matter and in a choice of difficulties, I would rather have Catholic youths in Protestant Colleges at Oxford with a strong Catholic Mission in the place, than a Catholic College.
(3) And I thought and think that the Bishops took an unadvisable steps and brought the whole Catholic body in England into a great difficulty, when on March 23 1865, they discountenanced, to the practical effect of a prohibition, the residence of Catholics in Oxford.'[1]

A little earlier Newman had written in a similar strain to Lord Howard of Glossop. 'On the whole I do not know how to avoid the conclusion that mixed education in the higher schools is as much a necessity now in England, as it was in the East in the days of St Basil and St Chrysostom.' Newman's conclusion was that

In a large University there are good and bad sets; and a youth has an opportunity of choosing between them. In a small exclusive body there is no choice; and one bad member ruins for a time the whole community. Thus the open University, when complemented by a strong Mission, may be even safer than a close Catholic College.[2]

In 1882, when there was a new Pope and Newman was a Cardinal, he encouraged Lord Braye to re-open in Rome the question of University education for Catholics. It was hoped to bring the matter before Leo XIII and to explain what a great opening for the good of religion was being lost at Oxford. The neglect, Newman wrote, 'is only one out of various manifestations of what may be called Nihilism in the Catholic Body, and in its rulers. They forbid, but they do not direct or create'.[3]

The blocking of higher education for Catholics on grounds that now seem to have had so little justification, and even to be ludicrous, was not the only example of ultramontane activity. The extremists were magnifying the prerogatives of the papacy, and introducing into England from the Continent exaggerated devotion to the Blessed Virgin. When an Anglican, Newman's mission had been to restore Revealed Religion in its integrity: now his duty lay in moderating excess. If unity was to be regained, Anglicanism

1. *Ward*, II, p. 555
2. 'Newman's Idea of an Educated Laity' by John Coulson, in *Theology and the University*, edited by the same, London 1964, p. 60
3. *Ward*, II, p. 486

must make good its deficiencies and Catholicism cut away its exaggerations. From the time of his first conversion in 1816, Newman had been praying for the restoration of unity among Christians. It was necessarily an underlying theme of the Tractarian movement. When in 1857 the enthusiastic Catholic convert Ambrose de Lisle and others founded the Association for the Promotion of the Unity of Christendom, to bring about corporate reunion, Newman did not join it. It seemed to him unwise to raise hopes which, in the staunchly Protestant England of that day, could not be realised. In answer to a pamphlet on reunion that de Lisle had sent him Newman wrote that he feared its tendency

> . . . to persuade individual Anglicans to wait out of communion with the Catholic Church, till they can come over with the others, in a body. There is such an extreme difficulty in rousing the mind to the real *necessity* of leaving the position into which men have grown up, their profession perhaps, their neighbourhood, or their family, or their work, that they will easily avail themselves of any slightest excuse—and even a hint from a person so deeply respected as yourself, so beloved, yourself too a convert, is more than sufficient to turn the scale, when the mind is in suspense. And then suppose, if these very dear and precious souls, say Dr. Pusey, are taken away in this state, when grace has been offered them, and they have not followed it up.
>
> I perfectly agree with you in thinking that the movement of 1833 is not over in this country, whatever be the state of Oxford itself; also I think if is for the *interest* of Catholicism that individuals should not join us, but should remain to leaven the mass,—I mean that they will do more for us by remaining where they are than by coming over, but then they have individual souls, and with what heart can I do anything to induce them to preach to others, if they themselves thereby become castaways?[1]

A few years later Newman wrote about corporate reunion to de Lisle: 'As a Protestant I never could get myself to entertain it as such, nor have I been able as a Catholic.'[2] It did not seem possible in the ordinary providence of God. Nevertheless, when in 1864 the Association for the Promotion of the Unity of Christendom was condemned at Rome, Newman wrote to de Lisle: 'For myself, I did not see my way to belong to the Union Association, but I think its members have been treated cruelly.'[3] It had been denounced by Manning, who had the support of extremist converts.

1. E. S. Purcell, *Life and Letters of Ambrose Phillipps de Lisle*, London 1900, I, p. 368 2. *Op. cit.*, II, pp. 264–5 3. *Ward*, II, p. 82

A year later Pusey published his *The Church of England a Portion of Christ's One Holy Catholic Church, and a Means of Restoring Visible Unity. An Eirenicon.* There he declared his view that exaggerated Catholic devotion to the Blessed Virgin was one of the chief obstacles to unity, another being excessive claims for papal infallibility (which was not yet defined as a doctrine of faith). Besides Manning, Faber and W. G. Ward (a married convert clergymen) were the chief promoters of these exaggerations. Newman thought Pusey's book unfair, and wrote to him that 'Eirenicon' seemed a misnomer, but he also disapproved strongly of the obstacles raised on the Catholic side. To the Jesuit Fr Coleridge he wrote on 24 November 1865: 'I think a large body in the Anglican Church are growing towards us, and, while I will not despair even of Pusey, however humanly unlikely, still less do I think it right to do any thing likely to throw back that large body. I cannot help feeling sorrow at the blow struck by the Holy Office at the members of the A.P.U.C. And if now, they are led to suppose that all Catholics hold with Ward and Faber, I think we shall in a melancholy way be seconding that blow.' Newman decided to reply to the *Eirenicon*, and to use the opportunity to dissociate Catholicism from the extremists.

The *Letter to Pusey on occasion of his Eirenicon* was published early in 1866. It began, 'No one who desires the union of Christendom after its many and long-standing divisions, can have any other feeling than joy, my dear Pusey, at finding from your recent Volume, that you see your way to make definite proposals to us for effecting that great object'. Of Pusey's followers Newman went on to say, 'I know the joy it would give those conscientious men of whom I am speaking, to be one with ourselves. I know how their hearts spring up with a spontaneous transport at the very thought of union'. Some of Pusey's statements, however, were both in manner and matter very wounding to Catholics. 'There was one of old time who wreathed his sword in myrtle; excuse me—you discharge your olive-branch as if from a catapult.'[1] Newman then went on to dissociate himself from Faber and Ward.

Though I am a convert, then, I think I have a right to speak out; and that the more because other converts have spoken for a long time, while I have not spoken; and with still more reason may I speak without

1. *Diff.*, II, pp. 1, 3 and 7

offence in the case of your present criticisms of us, considering that, in the charges you bring, the only two English writers you quote in evidence, are both of them converts, younger in age than myself. I put aside the Archbishop (Manning) of course, because of his office.

Newman then denied that Faber's views on our Lady and Ward's on papal infallibility were generally accepted. 'Our silence as regards their writings is very intelligible: it is not agreeable to protest, in the sight of the world, against the writings of men in our own Communion whom we love and respect.' Instead Newman appealed to the teaching of the old English Catholics, and also said: 'I prefer English habits of belief and devotion to foreign, from the same causes, and by the same right, which justifies foreigners in preferring their own.'[1] As regards our Lady, Newman appealed to the Fathers who 'made me a Catholic'. He showed that the moderate Catholic teaching about her hardly differed from theirs, who called her 'Mother of God, Second Eve, and Mother of all Living . . . the All-undefiled Mother of holiness', and concluded that 'the line cannot be logically drawn between the teaching of the Fathers concerning the Blessed Virgin and our own'.[2] As to the extreme exaggerations, some of them quite shocking, which Pusey had unearthed, Newman said: 'Sentiments such as these I freely surrender to your animadversion; I never knew of them till I read your book, nor, as I think, do the vast majority of English Catholics know them.' These last welcomed the real devotion to our Lady which the *Letter to Pusey* described with the warmth of personal conviction, but which, of course, allowed no comparison with her Son.

He alone has an entrance into our soul, reads our secret thoughts, speaks to our heart, applies to us spiritual pardon and strength. On Him we solely depend. He alone is our inward life. . . . Mary is only our mother by divine appointment, given us from the Cross; her presence is above not on earth; her office is external, not within us. Her name is not heard in the administration of the Sacraments. Her work is not one of ministrations towards us; her power is indirect. It is her prayers that avail, and her prayers are effectual by the *fiat* of Him who is our all in all.[3]

At the beginning of his *Letter to Pusey* Newman also maintained that Catholics and Anglicans did not really differ in their attitude

1. *Diff.*, II, pp. 20 and 22
2. *Diff.*, II, p. 78
3. *Diff.*, II, pp. 114 and 84

to Holy Scripture. Both insisted that the teachings of tradition must be taken into account in its interpretation. Catholics said that not every article of faith was so contained in Scripture 'that it may thence be logically proved, *independently* of the teaching and authority of tradition', Anglicans that every article of faith was contained in Scripture, '*provided* there be added the illustrations and compensations supplied by the *Tradition*'. Anglicans did not say 'that the whole revelation is in Scripture, in such sense that pure unaided logic can draw it from the sacred text', nor did Catholics say 'that it was not in Scripture, in an improper sense, in the sense that the *Tradition* of the Church is able to recognize and determine it there'.[1]

Having dealt with the question of our Lady, Newman left over that of Infallibility. A beginning had been made in dissociating Catholicism from the extremists: more harm than good might be done by discussing the subject during the feverish years preceding the First Vatican Council. Also one of Newman's Oratorians, the young Ignatius Ryder, was controverting with W. G. Ward on the subject, resisting his claim that all the doctrinal statements of the Pope were infallible. Newman, indeed, had already spoken about the Church's infallibility at the end of the *Apologia*. The years that followed were the last of the temporal power of the papacy, and the general sympathy for Pius IX made it easier for the ultramontanes to press on with their demands for a definition, which the Pope himself favoured. The extremists were speaking as though it would be laid down that infallibility covered all official utterances of the Pope. Such a claim had no basis in history and would soon have undermined the whole idea of a Revealed Religion, but it was very strongly pressed, and those who opposed it were harshly denounced as 'Gallicans'. Many Catholics, and by no means only converts, were very disturbed as to what might happen. Newman insisted to them on the limitations to infallibility which he had already laid down, and pointed out that a definition of papal infallibility would not involve believing more, but would merely settle more clearly the *seat* of infallibility—that is, what organs or authorities in the Church were protected from error when they solemnly expounded revealed doctrine. If the Pope was to be infallible it would only be because he was at the head of a Church that was such. Newman, from the time he

1. *Diff.*, II, p. 12

became a Catholic, had accepted the doctrine of papal infallibility on the authority of the Church. It had no difficulty in itself for him, but he considered it very inopportune to cause grave unease within the Church and animosity outside it by a definition. All the more since, in practice, the spiritual power of the papacy was being increasingly recognised and admitted by Catholics, and the process of centralisation concentrating government more and more in Rome. In this he was at one with all the more far-seeing and learned bishops at the Council, for intellectually and morally the 'inopportune' minority far outweighed the majority.

Before the Council it was suggested from Rome that Newman might be a Consultor on one of the preparatory Commissions. He weighed up the pros and cons and decided he ought to decline. His work (he was then writing *A Grammar of Assent*) would be seriously interrupted, he had never succeeded in working on boards or committees, could not make his presence felt among high ecclesiastics, knew no language but his own, and his health was not good. 'I have a warning, in the time I lost in Dublin of what will come of my throwing myself into a work foreign to my talents, and among strange persons.' The conclusion was, 'There are some things I *can* do, others I can't. I should, by accepting this invitation, lose my independence and gain nothing'. Mgr Dupanloup, the Bishop of Orleans, and a leading inopportunist later asked Newman to be his theologian at the Council, but the offer was declined for the same reasons.

Newman realised the danger of a definition being forced through by the extremists, which it would be difficult to reconcile with Revelation and with history. He did not see what he could do publicly to avert this, but at least he could urge the danger on his own bishop. Hence to Ullathorne at the Council, which had opened on 8 December 1869, he wrote on 28 January following what he later described as 'one of the most passionate and confidential letters that I ever wrote in my life':

Rome ought to be a name to lighten the heart at all times, and a Council's proper office is, when some great heresy or other evil impends, to inspire the faithful with hope and confidence. But now we have the greatest meeting which has ever been, and that at Rome, infusing into us by the accredited organs of Rome and its partisans (such as the *Civilità*, the *Armonia*, the *Univers*, and the *Tablet*) little else than fear and dismay. When we are all at rest and have no doubts, and, at least practically, not to say doctrinally, hold the Holy Father to be infallible, suddenly there is thunder in the clear sky, and we are told to prepare for something, we know not what, to try our faith, we know not how. No impending danger is to be averted, but a great difficulty is to be created. Is this the proper work for an Ecumenical Council? As to myself personally, please God, I do not expect any trial at all, but I cannot help suffering with the various souls which are suffering, and I look with anxiety at the prospect of having to defend decisions which may not be difficult to my private judgment, but may be most difficult to maintain logically in the face of historical facts. What have we done to be treated as the Faithful never were treated before? When has definition of doctrine *de fide* been a luxury of devotion and not a stern painful necessity? Why should an aggressive insolent faction be allowed to make the hearts of the just to mourn, whom the Lord hath not made sorrowful? Why can't we be let alone when we have pursued peace and thought no evil? I assure you, my dear Lord, some of the truest minds are driven one way and another, and do not know where to rest their feet; one day determining to give up all theology as a bad job and recklessly to believe henceforth almost that the Pope is impeccable; at another tempted to believe all the worst that a book like Janus says; at another doubting about the capacity possessed by Bishops drawn from all corners of the earth to judge what is fitting for European society, and then again angry with the Holy See for listening to the flattery of a clique of Jesuits, Redemptorists and converts. . . .

With these thoughts before me, I am continually asking myself whether I ought not to make my feelings public; but all I do is to pray those great early Doctors of the Church, whose intercession would decide the matter,—Augustine and the rest,—to avert so great a calamity. If it is God's Will that the Pope's Infallibility should be defined, then it is His Blessed Will to throw back 'the times and the moments' of that triumph He has destined for His Kingdom; and I shall feel I have but to bow my head to His Adorable Inscrutable Providence.[1]

Ullathorne showed this confidential letter to one or two other bishops, allowing it out of his hands for a few hours. Someone managed to copy it, and in March it appeared in full in the *Standard* newspaper. The letter had been entirely confidential, but in the end Newman was glad of its unlicensed publication. He had felt that his own views should be made public, but the subject was so complicated and required such careful statement that he had

1. *Ward*, II, pp. 287–8; Cuthbert Butler, *The Life and Times of Bishop Ullathorne*, II, pp. 58–9, a more accurate text.

been definitely dissuaded from writing on it. Now what his feelings were had come out, without any responsibility on his part. Eventually the doctrine was defined, in spite of strong opposition on the part of the bishops of some of the greatest sees, and thanks to what is now admitted to have been undue pressure on the part of Pius IX. Newman had all along feared that the extremists would rush it through without consideration of the facts of history or of the feelings of those who wished for more time to turn it over in all its aspects. The definition of the Immaculate Conception, after many centuries, amid general agreement, and after the consultation of the whole body of the Church, had been very different. Reasserting the principle he had illustrated in his article on the Laity, he insisted: 'The Church moves as a whole; it is not a mere philosophy, it is a communion; it not only discovers, but it teaches; it is bound to consult for charity as well as for faith.'[1]

The final form of the definition of papal infallibility was moderate enough, and although many felt it to be inopportune, it was in the course of three years accepted by all the Catholic bishops. In fact the form of the definition was in reality something of a defeat for the extremists. It was nonetheless an over-emphasis in one direction, always a dangerous thing when revealed truth is at stake. Newman spent much time in the years after 1870 reassuring and explaining matters to the many Catholics who were disturbed in their faith by what had happened. To Mrs William Froude he wrote:

> I have no hesitation in saying that, to all appearance, Pius IX wished to say a great deal more (that is that the Council should say a great deal more) than it did, but a greater power hindered it. A Pope is not inspired; he has not an inherent gift of divine knowledge. When he speaks *ex cathedra*, he may say little or much, but he is simply protected from saying what is untrue.[2]

To Miss Holmes he wrote prophetically:

> We must have a little faith. Abstract propositions avail little . . . no truth stands by itself—each is kept in order and harmonized by other truths. The dogmas relative to the Holy Trinity and the Incarnation were not struck off all at once—but piecemeal—one Council did one thing, another a second—and so the whole dogma was built up. And the first portion of it looked extreme—and controversies rose upon it

1. *Ward*, II, p. 296 2. *Ward*, II, p. 378

—and these controversies led to the second, and third Councils, and they did not *reverse* the first, but *explained* and *completed* what was first done. So it will be now. Future Popes will explain and in one sense limit their own power.[1]

Eventually Newman was given the opportunity to speak publicly and deliberately. In 1874 Gladstone was defeated over his Irish University Bill and forced to resign. He attributed his fall to the influence of the Irish bishops over Catholic members of Parliament, and came to the conclusion that after the definition of 1870 Catholics could no longer be loyal citizens. In fact, as Newman was to point out, the Irish bishops had been guided by their nationalism rather than by their Catholicism. In November, Gladstone published a pamphlet of which, by the end of the year, nearly 150,000 copies were sold, *The Vatican Decrees in their bearing on Civil Allegiance*. Newman's friends strongly urged him to reply, but one difficulty was that Gladstone had written as though the Infallibility Definition had taken over and promulgated the extreme views of Manning and Ward. Were Newman to deal with the question he must speak plainly. 'If I am to write, I will say my say.' That meant dissociating the Catholic Church from extreme views, as he had done about the Blessed Virgin in the *Letter to Pusey*, and in effect attacking Archbishop Manning and Ward. Newman was reluctant, but felt, 'I was bound to write from my duty to those many men who had been more or less influenced in their conversion by my own conversion—and whom I fancied saying to me, "Is this what you have let us in for" '.[2] The result was *A Letter addressed to the Duke of Norfolk on occasion of Mr Gladstone's Recent Expostulation*, written at the end of 1874, in Newman's best manner, within a few weeks of his seventy-fourth birthday. The Duke of Norfolk was a friend, like his father before him, and had been educated at Newman's school. He was the leading Catholic layman, and immediately touched by the slur on Catholic patriotism. In the preface, Newman laid blame on the extremists for the severity with which Gladstone had spoken.

I own to a deep feeling, that Catholics may in good measure thank themselves, and no one else, for having alienated from them so religious a mind. There are those among us, as it must be confessed, who for years past have conducted themselves as if no responsibility

1. *Ward*, II, p. 379 2. *Ward*, II, p. 405

attached to wild words and overbearing deeds; who have stated truths in the most paradoxical form, and stretched principles till they were close upon snapping; and who at length, having done their best to set the house on fire, leave to others the task of putting out the flame.[1]

Newman returned to this towards the end of his *Letter*:

What I felt deeply, and ever shall feel, while life lasts, is the violence and cruelty of journals and other publications, which, taking as they professed to do the Catholic side, employed themselves by their rash language (though, of course, they did not mean it so), in unsettling the weak in faith, throwing back inquirers, and shocking the Protestant mind. Nor do I speak of publications only; a feeling was too prevalent in many places that no one could be true to God and His Church, who had any pity on troubled souls, or any scruple of 'scandalizing those little ones who believed in' Christ, and of 'despising and destroying him for whom He died'.[2]

In replying to Gladstone, Newman relied on the principles which had governed his life all through. Gladstone accused Catholics of 'repudiating ancient history'. Newman appealed to the practice of the Church of the Fathers in regards to the limits of the obedience due to the State.

Go through the long annals of Church History, century after century and say, was there ever a time when her Bishops, and notably the Bishop of Rome, were slow to give their testimony in behalf of the moral and revealed law and to suffer for their obedience to it? ever a time when they forgot that they had a message to deliver to the world,—not the task merely of administering spiritual consolation, or of making the sick bed easy, . . . but specially and directly a definite message to high and low, from the world's Maker . . .?

That remained always the Church's great offence. Newman went on to point the lesson of Tractarianism:

In truth, this fidelity to the ancient Christian system, seen in modern Rome, was the luminous fact which more than any other turned men's minds at Oxford forty years ago to look towards her with reverence, interest, and love. It affected individual minds variously of course; some it even brought on eventually to conversion, others it only restrained from active opposition to her claims; but none of us could read the Fathers, and determine to be their disciples, without feeling that Rome, like a faithful steward, had kept in fulness and in vigour what our own communion had let drop. The Tracts for the Times

1. *Diff.*, II, pp. 176–7 2. *Diff.*, II, p. 300

were founded on a deadly antagonism to what in these last centuries has been called Erastianism or Caesarism.[1]

Newman then maintained that nowhere were the powers exercised by the bishops of the fourth century still in full action except in the Catholic Church. 'We must either give up the belief in the Church as a divine institution altogether, or we must recognise it in this day in that communion of which the Pope is the head. . . . We must take things as they are; to believe in a Church, is to believe in the Pope.' And Newman insisted about Gladstone: 'It is not the existence of a Pope, but of a Church, which is his aversion. It is the powers themselves, and not their distribution and allocation in the ecclesiastical body which he writes against.'[2] It was the New Testament itself which laid down that the rulers of the Church were to be obeyed.

And surely this is what every one of us will say as well as the Pope, who is not an Erastian, and who believes that the Gospel is no mere philosophy thrown upon the world at large, no mere quality of mind and thought, no mere beautiful and deep sentiment or subjective opinion, but a substantive message from above, guarded and preserved in a visible polity.[3]

Yet, although the authorities of the Church received guidance from the Holy Spirit, they did not always obey it fully, and definitions could be one-sided and in need of correction, owing to the quality of the men who met together in a Council. The Holy Spirit hindered definite error, but not the lesser consequences of human frailty.[4]

Towards the end of his *Letter* Newman returned to the accusation that the Church repudiated history, and treated once more of the relations between history and dogma. He referred with great respect to Döllinger and his followers, who rejected the 1870 definition on historical grounds, and left Catholic communion in consequence. Newman denied 'not their report of facts, but their use of the facts they report'. To him it seemed that they expected 'from History more than History can furnish and to have too little confidence in the Divine Promise and Providence' which guarded the definitions of Popes and Councils.

1. *Diff.*, II, pp. 197–8
2. *Diff.*, II, pp. 207–10
3. *Diff.*, II, p. 236
4. *Diff.*, II, pp. 307–8

For myself, I would simply confess that no doctrine of the Church can be rigorously proved by historical evidence: but at the same time that no doctrine can be simply disproved by it. Historical evidence reaches a certain way, more or less, towards a proof of the Catholic doctrines; often nearly the whole way; sometimes it goes only as far as to point in their direction . . . in all cases there is a margin left for the exercise of faith in the word of the Church. He who believes the dogmas of the Church only because he has reasoned them out of History, is scarcely a Catholic.[1]

Newman then went on to speak of the Infallibility definition itself, and to explain that the Church took the greatest care to contract the range of those truths, to which, as included in the original divine revelation, the assent of faith must be given. This was her charitable duty, but, alas, 'a few years ago it was the fashion among us to call writers, who conformed to this rule of the Church, by the name of "Minimizers"; that day of tyrannous *ipse dixits*, I trust, is over'. To the Church had been entrusted the revealed message, and 'so far as the message entrusted to it is concerned, the Church is infallible; for what is meant by infallibility in teaching but that the teacher in his teaching is secured from error?' 'To the Apostles the whole revelation was given, by the Church it is transmitted; no simply new truth has been given to us since St John's death; the one office of the Church is to guard "that noble deposit" of truth, as St Paul speaks to Timothy, which the Apostles bequeathed to her, in its fulness and integrity. Hence the infallibility of the Apostles was of a far more positive and wide character than that needed by and granted to the Church. We call it, in the case of the Apostles, inspiration, in the case of the Church, *assistentia*.' The 'principle of minimizing' was necessary 'for a wise and cautious theology'. 'To be a true Catholic a man must have a generous loyalty towards ecclesiastical authority, and accept what is taught him with what is called the *pietas fidei*', but 'such a tone of mind has a claim . . . to be met and handled with a wise and gentle *minimism*'.[2]

Newman met the accusation that Catholics were divided in their allegiance by an exposition of which Harold Laski wrote, in the *Problem of Sovereignty*, that it 'remains with some remarks of Sir Henry Maine and a few brilliant dicta of F. W. Maitland as perhaps the profoundest discussion of the nature of obedience and

1. *Diff.*, II, pp. 311–12 2. *Diff.*, II, pp. 321, 323, 327, 332, 339

of sovereignty to be found in the English language'.[1] Newman pointed out that the State, as well as the Church, had the power of imposing its will on us and circumscribing our liberties. The Pope interfered far less in our private affairs than the State, and in fact neither interfered 'either with our comfort or our consciences'. Extreme cases could occur, however, and then it would be seen that obedience could never be absolute. Allegiance to the Sovereign power, whether civil or ecclesiastical, depended on and was ultimately limited by the dictates of conscience. This led Newman on to speak of the supreme authority of conscience, which for him 'is the voice of God, whereas it is fashionable on all hands now to consider it in one way or another a creation of man'. He made his appeal to all Christians: 'When Anglicans, Wesleyans, the various Presbyterian sects in Scotland, and other denominations among us, speak of conscience, they mean what we mean, the voice of God in the nature and heart of man, as distinct from the voice of Revelation . . . it is a messenger from Him, who both in nature and in grace, speaks to us behind a veil, and teaches and rules us by His representatives. Conscience is the aboriginal Vicar of Christ, a prophet in its informations, a monarch in its peremptoriness, a priest in its blessings and anathemas.' This was very different from the right to do or believe what one pleased. For many people freedom of conscience meant the right 'to dispense with conscience, to ignore a Lawgiver and a Judge, to be independent of unseen obligations'. Conscience in its true sense was the foundation of the Pope's authority, and it would be suicidal in him to speak against it. His power came from Revelation, which supplied the insufficiences of the natural light of conscience, and 'the championship of the Moral Law and of conscience is his *raison d être*'.[2] But what if there were a direct conflict between the teaching of the Pope and the clear prompting of conscience. This could only happen if the Pope legislated or gave orders, and Newman was quite clear that the man who, after praying and taking counsel, was convinced that such laws or orders were immoral, must disobey them. He cited various Catholic authorities in confirmation of this, beginning with the declaration of the Fourth Lateran Council, 'He who acts against his conscience loses his soul'. Newman concluded thus: 'I add one remark.

1. Harold J. Laski, *Studies in the Problem of Sovereignty*, London 1917, p. 202
2. *Diff.*, II, pp. 247–8, 250, 253

Certainly, if I am obliged to bring religion into after-dinner toasts (which indeed does not seem quite the thing), I shall drink—to the Pope, if you please,—still—to Conscience first, and to the Pope afterwards.'[1]

A Letter to the Duke of Norfolk was acclaimed on all sides when it appeared, and it remains a work of permanent value. Not only the converts, but the old Catholics, including Bishops and Jesuits, were delighted with it. Cullen, now a Cardinal, praised it in a pastoral. Anglicans welcomed its straightforwardness and its rejection of extreme ultramontanism. Gladstone in his reply praised Newman's 'kindliness of tone', and 'the admissions, which such integrity, combined with such acuteness, has not been able to withhold'. He paid a tribute to Newman's importance for the religious history of England, and to 'the perhaps ill-appreciated greatness of his early life and works. . . . All he produces is and must be most notable. But has he outrun, has he overtaken the greatness of the "History of the Arians" and of the "Parochial Sermons", those indestructable classics of English theology?'[2] At Rome, where Newman's *Letter* had been denounced as censurable, they were not so pleased. When Manning was approached from Propaganda, he wrote back that 'The heart of the revered Fr Newman is as right and as Catholic as it is possible to be', and that reasons of prudence made silence essential. Anything like a public censure would do the greatest harm, and the English ultramontanes would be blamed for it. Ullathorne, who was also written to, replied in the same way, but towards the end of 1875, perhaps thanks to further protests by English ultramontanes, he was again asked to elicit some public correction from Newman. Ullathorne was not to say he had received instructions from Rome, but speak to him as though on his own. Ullathorne had had enough of trying to deal 'blandly and suavely' with Newman, on secret orders from Propaganda, and replied: 'Fr Newman has often complained that the authorities at Rome do not deal with him directly and openly, but by intermediaries and secretly. I strongly urge that if anything is to be done, he be written to directly and openly.' That seems to have been the end of the matter. The more serious Roman complaints were based on a misunderstanding of what was maintained in the *Letter*, others objected to

1. *Diff.*, II, pp. 259–61
2. W. E. Gladstone, *Vaticanism*, London 1875, pp. 11–12

what was said about the failure of Clement VII's excommunication of Henry VIII and St Pius V's of Elizabeth, and to other strictures on Popes. Newman's remark that 'the Rock of St. Peter on its summit enjoys a pure and serene atmosphere, but there is a great deal of Roman *malaria* at the foot of it' was held to refer to the Roman Curia and the counsellors of Pius IX and to be 'troppo irreverente'.[1]

At the same time as he wrote the *Letter* Newman arranged for Ambrose St John to translate from the German, *True and False Infallibility*, by Monsignor Fessler, who had been Secretary-General of the Vatican Council. Fessler took a very moderate view of the scope of the Definition, and his book had received the approval of Pius IX. The translation reinforced the work of the *Letter*, but put too great a strain on Ambrose St John, who was all the time Headmaster of the Oratory School. He died in May 1875. Newman's grief was intense, for he had been a most faithful friend, and was the only one left at the Oratory who had been with him since the Littlemore days.

1. Cuthbert Butler, *The Life and Times of Bishop Ullathorne*, II, pp. 100–6. *Diff.*, II, p. 297

CHAPTER 9

A Grammar of Assent

THE years after the *Apologia* were by no means all taken up with the controversies over higher education for Catholics, the place of our Lady, and Papal Infallibility. Besides Newman's everyday priestly work, in his church of the Oratory and in his Oratory School, he found time to write his longest and most successful poem and the last of his full-scale treatises. After the poems at the time of the Mediterranean journey, collected in *Lyra Apostolica*, Newman had written very little poetry. As a Catholic he wrote a few hymns, chiefly in honour of our Lady and of St Philip. 'St Philip in his School' was in sapphics, and included the verses:

> This is the Saint, who, when the world allures us,
> Cries her false wares, and opes her magic coffers,
> Points to a better city, and secures us,
> With richer offers.
>
> Love is his bond, he knows no other fetter,
> Asks not our all, but takes what e'er we spare him,
> Willing to draw us on from good to better,
> As we can bear him.[1]

Now, suddenly, in January 1865, *The Dream of Gerontius* was written. He told a friend afterwards: 'it came into my head to write it, I really can't tell how. And I wrote on till it was finished, on small bits of paper, and I could no more write anything else by willing it than I could fly.' The poem is a description of the moment of death, followed by judgment and then entry into purgatory, all vividly realised. It was published first in the *Month*, May and June 1865. It attracted attention at once, and has retained it. Edward Elgar's musical setting was first performed in 1900. It is a sign of Newman's appeal that General Gordon read and marked the poem during his last days at Khartoum in 1882.

1. *Verses on Various Occasions*, p. 310, and for 'The Dream of Gerontius', pp. 323–70

Early in 1870 Newman published *A Grammar of Assent*, which he had been trying to compose, making numerous drafts, for twenty years. All his other works had been written in answer to some external call, for what may be called pastoral reasons, for some immediate religious purpose. He himself noted:

What I have written has been for the most part what may be called official, works done in some office I held or engagement I had made—all my Sermons are such, my Lectures on the Prophetical Office, on Justification, my Essays in the British Critic and translation of St Athanasius—or has been from some especial call, or invitation, or necessity, or emergency, as my Arians, Anglican Difficulties, Apologia or Tales. The Essay on Assent is nearly the only exception . . . I had felt it on my conscience for years, that it would not do to quit the world without doing it.[1]

Newman wanted to find the answer to a crucial problem, he wished to justify men's right to be certain, and especially their right to certitude in matters of religion. At the beginning of *Proper Studies*, Aldous Huxley acknowledged his debt to Newman, 'whose analysis of the psychology of thought remains one of the most acute, as it is certainly the most elegant, which has ever been made'. Nevertheless, Newman has puzzled many readers of *A Grammar of Assent*. He plunges at once into his subject without a word of introduction to show what he is trying to do. Fortunately he did explain his purpose elsewhere. Thus, for instance, he had a conversation, on 3 December 1877, with Edward Caswall the hymn-writer, one of his Oratorians, who afterwards noted down on the fly-leaf of his own copy of *A Grammar of Assent* the gist of what Newman had told him. 'Object of the book twofold. In the first part shows that you can believe what you cannot understand. In the second part that you can believe what you cannot absolutely prove.'

Part I of *A Grammar*, then, is not concerned directly with the problem of certitude but with showing, against Evangelicals and latitudinarians, the importance and value of doctrinal statements in religion. Newman takes up the defence of theology, and shows that so far from being antagonistic to vital religion, there can be no sound Christianity without it. It is an abstract, logical science, but it makes clear for us the truths on which our religion must rest.

1. *A.W.*, pp. 272–3

It can be a merely intellectual science without the life of religion, but it need not be. Its formulas elucidate for the worshipper the Object on which his imagination and affections rest. Devotion is protected by dogma. On the other hand, what is real is particular, and theology deals with general notions. It merely holds a truth in the intellect, whereas faith gives a real assent to a concrete reality, which is appropriated by the imagination and the heart. Newman then proceeds to show how, leaving aside Revelation, we can give a vivid assent to the being of God far stronger than we give to a mere notion of the intellect. He argues from our sense of moral obligation and shows how conscience is the connecting principle between the creature and his Creator. It brings us into His presence as a Living Person. These pages in *A Grammar* are Newman's clearest exposition of this fundamental theme: how, by means of our conscience, we come to hold as a great religious fact or reality that there is One Personal and Present God. He insists that the proposition ' "There is a God", when really apprehended, is the object of a strong energetic adhesion, which works a revolution in the mind; but when held merely as a notion, it requires but a cold and ineffective acceptance, though it be held ever so unconditionally'.[1]

In a similar way, he maintains of the doctrine of the Holy Trinity, professed in the Creeds, concerning the Father, from Whom are and ever have been the Son and the Holy Spirit, that it deals not with abstractions but with realities, and on them our spiritual life is built. First he expounds the doctrine that the One Personal God

> . . . at once is Father, is Son, is Holy Ghost, each of whom is that one Personal God in the fulness of His Being and Attributes; so that the Father is all that is meant by the word 'God', as if we knew nothing of Son or of Spirit; and in like manner the Son and the Spirit are Each by Himself all that is meant by the word, as if the Other Two were unknown; moreover, that by the word 'God' is meant nothing over and above what is meant by 'the Father', or by 'the Son', or by 'the Holy Ghost', and that the Father is in no sense the Son, nor the Son the Holy Ghost, nor the Holy Ghost the Father. Such is the prerogative of the Divine Infinitude, that that One and Single Personal Being, the Almighty God, is really Three, while He is absolutely One.[2]

1. *G.A.*, p. 126
2. *G.A.*, p. 125

Newman remarks of that exposition that there are no scientific terms in it. The word 'Personal', 'though it cannot mean precisely the same when used of God as when used of man', yet is sufficiently explained by its ordinary use to allow of its being intelligibly applied to the Divine Nature. The other words which occur in this account of the Holy Trinity—Three, One, He, God, Father, Son, Spirit—are none of them words peculiar to theology. They have a popular meaning, and are used according to that obvious popular meaning to explain the doctrine. No human words are adequate, but those ones are among the simplest and most intelligible to be found in language. It is on each of those propositions, taken one by one, that the devotion and spiritual life of the Christian rests, be he philosopher, child or peasant. It is only indirectly and when a man reflects on the propositions and begins to combine them, that he acknowledges the Doctrine to be a Mystery. Its mysteriousness is not directly speaking intrinsic to the doctrine. The Mystery expresses a notion, not a thing, and is matter for theology rather than religion, though the devout mind may lovingly welcome it as befitting the Incomprehensibility of the Supreme Being.

Newman concludes:

Break a ray of light into its constituent colours, each is beautiful, each may be enjoyed; attempt to unite them, and perhaps you produce only a dirty white. The pure and indivisible Light is seen only by the blessed inhabitants of heaven; here we have but such faint reflections of it as its diffraction supplies; but they are sufficient for faith and devotion. Attempt to combine them into one, and you gain nothing but a mystery, which you can describe as a notion, but cannot depict as an imagination.

Thus the doctrine of the Holy Trinity in Unity is never described as a mystery in Scripture, 'which is addressed far more to the imagination and affections than to the intellect'. Nor is it described as a mystery in the Creeds, which have the nature of prayers, and where intellectual difficulties would be out of place. The Athanasian Creed, especially, the chief part of which sets forth the doctrine, is called a 'psalm' and is no mere collection of notions. Newman remarks: 'For myself, I have ever felt it as the most simple and sublime, the most devotional formulary to which Christianity has given birth, more so even than the *Veni Creator* and the *Te Deum*.'[1] How different are the theological textbooks and

1. *G.A.*, pp. 132–3

the catechisms which insist continually on the mysteriousness of the doctrine. They systematise and give a noti nal assent to the whole, whereas the New Testament, and especia y St John and St Paul, provide us with separate propositions, to any one of which we can give a real assent. They speak continually of Father, Son and Holy Spirit, but always in a way that is concrete and particular. 'Hence theology has to do with the Dogma of the Holy Trinity as a whole made up of many propositions; but Religion has to do with each of those separate propositions which compose it, and lives and thrives in the contemplation of them.'[1]

It is in Part II of *A Grammar of Assent* that Newman deals with his basic problem, certitude, and above all certitude in matters of religion. His purpose is, as he told Father Caswall, to show 'that you can believe what you cannot absolutely prove'. Newman was writing to counter rationalism, and to explain how faith, whether in the sphere of religion or of ordinary life, was a reasonable act, even when not based on strictly scientific demonstration. He had in mind two distinct classes of people. First there were the educated, the high-minded Victorian agnostics and rationalists. They were taught, in matters of importance, only to assent after proof, and to regard it as an offence against the truth, to accept more than was demonstrated. The acceptance of beliefs which could not be demonstrated in proper form must take rank below convictions established by science. This tension Newman had experienced from the beginning of his life, but it was made agonising for him when he saw it as a living reality in the minds of his friends. He felt it especially in the case of Hurrell Froude's brother, William, who had become an agnostic, and whom Newman hoped, in vain as it turned out, to bring to the acceptance of the Catholic faith. It was to convince such men that he wrote *A Grammar of Assent*. Eleven years before its publication, Froude wrote to Newman that 'even the highest attainable probability does not justify the mind in discarding the residuum of doubt', and that to attempt to tip the balance by any other than rational considerations, 'is distinctly an immoral use of faculties'.[2]

Besides the educated agnostics there was the other category Newman had in mind, the vast majority of mankind, who believed

1. *G.A.*, p. 140
2. Gordon Huntington Harper, *Cardinal Newman and William Froude*, Baltimore 1933, p. 120

truths which they were quite incapable either of explaining satisfactorily or defending l gically. In their case, too, it was necessary to show that they were justified in believing what they could not absolutely prove. The ordinary simple Christian, the charcoal-burner, had, until Newman appeared, found few to defend his right to believe without logical proof. Newman came to grips with a burning problem which earlier theologians had not really faced. St Thomas Aquinas sketches the evidence for Christianity in the famous apologetic chapters at the beginning of the *Contra Gentes*. He lists some of the clearest arguments for its divine origin, as a proof that a Christian 'non leviter credit', 'does not lightly believe'. Newman, in his copy, marked a number of passages, and his pencilled comment at this point may still be read: 'He who believes "non leviter credit" not because he knows there are, but because there are weighty evidences.' St Thomas was concerned primarily with the objective justification of faith in mysteries, Newman had the more complicated and practical aim of vindicating the right of the ignorant man to believe in mysteries, the evidence for which he had never studied. He proposed to defend the mass of the faithful against the accusation that they were fideists. The apologists of the day naively remarked that it was not difficult to understand how learned people could judge with certainty that they ought to believe in the Christian Revelation; the difficulty was to see how the simple and uneducated could do so. Yet we are told that Christ came to preach the Gospel to the poor, and to reveal mysteries that were hidden from the wise and prudent to little ones, and it is usually these who find it easiest to have firm faith. Newman himself, in one of the many drafts of the *Grammar*, sketched out this problem—how could ordinary people, whose duty it was to accept the Christian Faith, have sufficient proof to make their acceptance of it reasonable?

January 5. 1860. On the popular, practical, personal evidence for the truth of revelation. I am not here to dispute that the alleged fact of the supernatural origin of Christianity ought to be subjected to the same rigorous cross-examination, and ought to satisfy the same logical criticism of truth, which are applied in the case of secular sciences. . . . Nor am I disputing the assertion of theologians that such an ordeal is actually met, undergone, and satisfied by Christianity . . . I am addressing myself to a question . . . demanding a decision in the affirmative, viz., that the *motivum credibilitatis* is personal to each individual as well as formal, public, and what may be called objective. . . . Such individual conviction cannot rise from grounds altogether separate from the logical and formal body of evidence; it must be concurrent with and included in that moral and scientific proof. However it is *sui generis* and varying with the individual. By the scientific proof I mean the arguments from miracles, from prophecy, etc, etc, . . . If I speak of this it will be but incidentally; for I am aiming at meeting an objection which is at once most obvious and most frequently urged, and most plausible, and which has great weight with people just now. . . . The great mass of Catholics know nothing of argument, how then is their faith rational? The peasant believes 'what he is told', and if his priest told him that the Holy Ghost was incarnate, he would have faith in that heresy. Catholics are forbidden to reconsider the truth of their faith. . . . Now is not this a clear token that Catholicism is not proved in the sense that other facts, other sciences are proved? If they are so certain, as they say, what harm can listening to objections do them? . . . If they are afraid thus cordially to consider objections . . . it is a proof that after all they are not certain, and have but worked their mind into a persuasion . . . And that this is really the case, is plain from the undeniable fact that few persons have submitted to the Catholic Church upon a demonstration of her divinity; but merely upon those chance arguments and mere probabilities which came in his way. How can his belief be called rational? How can his treatment of his intellect be called honest? . . . I propose to draw out the nature of the evidence . . . on which individuals believe . . . what is meant by personal proof, giving instances, e.g. Mrs L. comes and says, 'I want to be a Catholic'. Her catechist is frightened, for he can find no motivum. . . . A factory girl comes and can only say, 'So and so brought me', etc, . . . a boy comes and says he wishes to get his sins forgiven.

Newman's aim then, was to vindicate the right of the ordinary man, and especially the simple, unlearned one, to assent to and have certitude about truths which he never had, and probably never could demonstrate. It must be made clear at once that *A Grammar of Assent* is not a treatise on the theory of knowledge, a manual of epistemology. It is, as Aldous Huxley realised, rather a book of psychology. Again and again Newman insisted, 'Abstract argument is always dangerous. . . . I prefer to go by facts'. 'We are in a world of facts, and we use them; for there is nothing else to use. . . . If I may not assume that I exist, and in a particular way, that is, with a particular mental constitution, I have nothing to speculate about, and had better let speculation alone.' 'We act according to our nature, by means of ourselves, when we remember or reason. We are as little able to accept or reject our mental constitution as our being.'[1] For all practical purposes the philosophy of the *Grammar* is that of common sense, of the plain man, of the philosopher when he is not philosophising, but occupied with the ordinary affairs of life. Further, if we may assume that Providence has made us as we are, we are more than ever justified in going by facts. At all events it is clear that the *Grammar* is not an ordinary philosophical treatise. Thus Newman wrote:

Earnestly maintaining . . . the certainty of knowledge, I think it enough to appeal to the common voice of mankind in proof of it. That is to be accounted a normal operation of our nature, which men in general do actually instance. That is a law of our minds, which is exemplified in action on a large scale, whether *à priori* it ought to be a law or no . . . our possession of certitude is a proof that it is not a weakness or an absurdity to be certain. How it comes about that we can be certain is not my business to determine; for me it is sufficient that certitude is felt. This is what the schoolmen, I believe, call treating a subject *in facto esse*, in contrast with *in fieri*. Had I attempted the latter, I should have been falling into metaphysics; but my aim is of a practical character . . . without excluding, far from it, the question of duty, I would confine myself to the truth of things, and to the mind's certitude of that truth.[2]

Newman, when he wished, could defend himself against idealism and scepticism, as the following quotation from his Philosophical Notebook suggests:

You can reduce me to a state of absolute scepticism about everything external to consciousness—but this is a reductio ad absurdum of all knowledge external to us whatever, of *senses* as well as (*I* should say *much more* than) supersensuous knowledge—but if you do not go to *this extreme length*, which makes it hopeless even to reason or investigate at all, you must allow *something*—and all I ask you to allow is *this*—that it is true that *I am*—or that my consciousness that I am represents the fact external to my consciousness (viz.) of my existence. Now see what is involved in this one assumption. Viz. My consciousness that I am is not *immediate*, but indirect. 'Sentio, ergo sum.' In this is involved therefore the presence of a faculty by which from what I have experience of, I argue the certainty of that of which I have not experience, viz. my existence, my existence being a fact external to consciousness.

This shows that Newman could have ruffled it with the best epistemologists, if he had wished. It is clear from the Notebook

1. *G.A.*, pp. 346–7; 61 2. *G.A.*, p. 344

that Newman had been planning a large work on metaphysics, which he abandoned after the *Rambler* delation. Instead, he confined himself to justifying certitude, the *sine qua non* of real religion. 'Without certitude in religious faith there may be much decency of profession and of observance, but there can be no habit of prayer, no directness of devotion, no intercourse with the unseen, no generosity of self-sacrifice. Certitude then is essential to the Christian; and if he is to preserve to the end, his certitude must include in it a principle of persistence.' And again: 'If religion is to be devotion, and not a mere matter of sentiment, if it is to be made the ruling principle of our lives, if our actions, one by one, and our daily conduct, are to be consistently directed towards an Invisible Being, we need something higher than a mere balance of arguments to fix and control our minds. Sacrifice of wealth, name, or position, faith and hope, self-conquest, communion with the spiritual world, presuppose a real hold and habitual intuition of the objects of Revelation, which is certitude under another name.'[1] As Newman asked in the *Apologia*: 'Who can really pray to a Being, about whose existence he is seriously in doubt?'

How, then, does Newman solve his problem? How are we to justify the ordinary assents and certitudes of life, the vast majority of which have neither resulted from nor can be proved by strict logic? Can we be certain of what we can neither perceive with our senses, nor prove mathematically? Is it permissible to accept and believe what we cannot absolutely prove? In *A Grammar of Assent* Newman gives his final answer to these questions, one which he had adumbrated thirty years earlier in his *Sermons preached before the University of Oxford*. Then he had distinguished between explicit and implicit reasoning, now called formal and informal inference. Formal inference is that verbal logic, with many limitations, which enables us to argue with others,

. . . something which may supersede the need of personal gifts by a far-reaching and infallible rule. Now without external symbols to mark out and to steady its course, the intellect runs wild, but with the aid of symbols, as in algebra, it advances with precision and effect. Let then our symbols be words: let all thought be arrested and embodied in words. Let language have a monopoly of thought, and thought go for only so much as it can show itself to be worth in language. Let every prompting of the intellect be ignored, every *momentum* of

1. *G.A.*, pp. 220, 238

argument be disowned, which is unprovided with an equivalent wording, as its ticket for sharing in the common search after truth. Let the authority of nature, commonsense, experience, genius, go for nothing. Ratiocination, thus restricted and put into grooves, is what I have called inference, and the science, which is its regulating principle, is logic.[1]

Newman insists that

Logic does not really prove; it enables us to join issue with others; it suggests ideas; it opens views; maps out for us the lines of thought; it verifies negatively; it determines where differences of opinion are hopeless; and when and how far conclusions are probable; but for genuine proof in concrete matter we require an *organon* more delicate, versatile, and elastic than verbal argumentation.[2]

And so,

. . . the processes of reasoning which legitimately lead to assent, to action, to certitude, are in fact too multiform, subtle, omnigenous, too implicit, to allow of being measured by rule, . . . they are after all personal,—verbal argumentation being useful only in subordination to a higher logic.[3]

This higher logic is informal and natural inference.

Our reasoning ordinarily presents itself to our mind as a simple act, not a process or series of acts. We apprehend the antecedent and then apprehend the consequent, without explicit recognition of the medium connecting the two, as if by a sort of direct association of the first thought with the second. We proceed by a sort of instinctive perception from premise to conclusion . . . instinctive . . . because ordinarily it acts by a spontaneous impulse, as prompt and inevitable as the exercise of sense and memory. . . . Such is ratiocination, in what may be called a state of nature, as it is found in the uneducated,—nay, in all men, in its ordinary exercise.[4]

'I say then,' Newman sums up, 'that our most natural mode of reasoning is, not from propositions to propositions, but from things to things, from concrete to concrete, from wholes to wholes.'[1] His position is that there is an implicit intellectual process, not opposed to conceptual reasoning, which gives complete and legitimate evidence, prior to any conceptual proof.

1. *G.A.*, p. 263
2. *G.A.*, p. 271
3. *G.A.*, p. 303
4. *G.A.*, pp. 259–60
5. *G.A.*, p. 330

Assent on reasonings not demonstrative is too widely recognized an act to be irrational, unless man's nature is irrational, too familiar to the prudent and clear-minded to be an infirmity or an extravagance. None of us can think or act without the acceptance of truths, not intuitive, not demonstrated, yet sovereign. If our nature has any constitution, any laws, one of them is this absolute reception of propositions as true, which lie outside the narrow range of conclusions to which logic, formal or virtual, is tethered; nor has any philosophical theory the power to force on us a rule which will not work for a day.[1]

It is the mind itself which controls its own reasonings, its informal and natural inferences, and not any technical apparatus of words and propositions. This power or faculty of judging and concluding, when perfected by experience, Newman called the illative sense. He compared it with the moral sense, which enables a person to decide what is right or wrong for him in given circumstances. An ethical system must be applied in a particular case. The illative sense is simply our intellect, or reason, sharpened by experience, working unconsciously, and arriving at its conclusions in an intellectual and reasonable manner. It has been defined as 'good sense', 'sound judgment', 'the intuitions of genius'. Newman called the 'illative sense' a solemn word for an ordinary thing. Any exercise of the judgment in coming to a conclusion, as distinct from the passive attention, which is all that is required in following a rigidly scientific proof, is an exercise of the illative sense. The illative sense is a purely intellectual faculty. A simple illustration of its working may be found in Willa Cather's novel about French Canada, *Shadows on the Rock*.

'When there is no sun, I can tell directions like the Indians.'

Here Auclair interrupted him, 'And how is that Antoine?'

Frichette smiled and shrugged. 'It is hard to explain, by many things. The limbs of the trees are generally bigger on the south side, for example. The moss on the trunks is clean and dry on the north side —on the south side it is softer and maybe a little rotten. There are many little signs; put them all together and they point you right.'

This heaping together of tiny indications, little facts, none of which, by itself, is conclusive, is what produces certitude in the mind. Those whose minds have been artificially disciplined according to a rigorously scientific and syllogistic method of ratiocination, find great difficulty in accepting this view. They

1. *G.A.*, p. 179

argue that probabilities can only lead to probabilities, and that a thousand probable arguments cannot produce certitude. More than a mere quantitative heaping up of probabilities is involved here. At a certain point there is a qualitative change. The indications corroborate each other, and produce something greater than themselves. Newman used the illustration of the '*cable*, which is made up of a number of separate threads, each feeble, yet together as sufficient as an iron rod. An iron rod represents mathematical or strict demonstration; a cable represents moral demonstration, which is an assemblage of probabilities, separately insufficient for certainty, but when put together, irrefragable'.[1] The illative sense cannot usually put its reasons into words, nor, since it is a personal gift or acquisition, can it act as a link between mind and mind. That is the business of logic, yet how seldom it is effective. If we really want to convince another, we try to avoid argument, we try to 'enter into his mind', to 'see his point of view', in order to discover what prevents him from seeing things as we do.

Newman, then, justifies the right of the ordinary man to his certitudes by appealing to the facts. 'We must take the constitution of the human mind as we find it, and not as we may judge it ought to be.' Men reason naturally and implicitly, and extract certitude from a host of probabilities. It is always dangerous to tamper with our minds, and to multiply the prerequisites of certitude. 'To meddle with the springs of thought and action is really to weaken them.'[1] To demand strict logical proof for the assents and certitudes, great and small, of life, is to ask that our minds should work unnaturally. That was the mistake of the eighteenth-century apologists for Christianity, and of the nineteenth-century agnostics, such as William Froude. It is analogous to the moral disease of scruples. It can be dangerous also, to rely unduly on discursive reasoning and the syllogism as a means of strengthening the faith of the young. Arguments against religion can appear more convincing and logical than the answers to them, and perhaps hardly admit of a reply in words at all. Hence it is often wiser to provide material on which the illative sense can work. If people are familiarised with Holy Scripture, the history or the Church, Christian biography, they soon realise where God is present and acting, and their faith has a firmer and broader foundation than logical argument could provide.

1. *Ward*, II, p. 43 2. *G.A.*, pp. 216–17

In his defence of the faith of the unlearned and of the right of the ordinary man to believe what he cannot prove, Newman made his appeal to the laws of human thought. On the title page of *A Grammar of Assent* he placed a sentence from St Ambrose, *Non in dialecticâ complacuit Deo salvum facere populum suum*, which he had quoted in his first book, *The Arians of the Fourth Century*, forty years before, and quoted again in the *Apologia*, when he remarked, 'I had a great dislike of paper logic'. In the *Grammar* he showed how logic deals with the notional and conceptual, when things are drained 'of that depth and breadth of associations which constitute their poetry, their rhetoric, and their historical life', and each term which represents them is starved down 'till it has become the ghost of itself, and everywhere one and the same ghost, so that it may stand for just one unreal aspect of the concrete thing to which it properly belongs, for a relation, a generalization, or other abstraction, for a notion neatly turned out of the laboratory of the mind, and sufficiently tame and subdued, because existing only in a definition'.[1] Since Newman's day there has been a reaction from conceptualism and rationalism, and many besides phenomenologists and existentialists acknowledge the primacy of the concrete and of personal experience.

Newman concluded *A Grammar of Assent* by applying his principles, and giving his outline of the evidences for Natural and Revealed Religion. Hence he began by laying down that 'egotism is true modesty'. In religious inquiry a man can only speak for himself. 'He knows what has satisfied and satisfies himself; if it satisfies him, it is likely to satisfy others.' These final chapters, Newman told a friend, were written 'especially for such ladies as are bullied by infidels and do not know how to answer them'. In them he illustrates his own fundamental principles, the necessity of moral dispositions for the search after truth, the importance of antecedent probability as the instrument of conviction, and the value of converging probabilities in building up a proof. His aim is to show that the Christian Revelation 'is a definite message from God to man distinctly conveyed by His chosen instruments, and to be received as such a message . . . not as probably true, or partially true, but as absolutely certain knowledge'.[2]

1. *G.A.*, p. 267
2. *G.A.*, pp. 384–7. Newman dealt with eternal punishment (pp. 399, 422, 502–3). He 'tried in various ways to make that truth less terrible to the intellect'. *Apo.*, p. 6. Cf. *Callista*, pp. 216–21

CHAPTER 10

Last Labours (1875-90)

ABOUT the time *A Grammar of Assent* appeared, Newman wrote to the Dominican nuns at Stone in Staffordshire on the subject of the *Life* they had just published of their saintly foundress and his great friend, Mother Margaret Mary Hallahan. They regretted that it did not seem to have effected many conversions. Newman replied:

> . . . there are two reasons for writing distinct from conversion, and, considering all things, I prefer them to any other reason—the one is to edify Catholics. Catholics are so often *raw*. Many do not know their religion—many do not know the reasons for it [i.e. the purpose of it]. . . . The other end which is so important, is what I call levelling up. If we are to convert souls savingly they must have the due preparation of heart, and if England is to be converted there must be a great move of the national mind to a better sort of religious sentiment. Wesleyans, Anglicans, Congregationalists, Unitarians, must be raised to one and the same (what we used to call at Oxford) 'ethos'. That is the same moral and intellectual state of mind. To bring them to this is 'levelling up'.

In 1863 Newman noted down in his private Journal the same idea or principle in other words, namely 'that the Church must be prepared for converts as well as converts prepared for the Church'.[1] One way of effecting this was to republish his Anglican sermons, which could thus serve a double irenical purpose. He was already planning this republication when the *Apologia* came along to strengthen his position and also his financial resources. There could be no question of trying to 'catholicise' the sermons, as he had been persuaded to do in the case of his fourth volume. People would only read Newman unexpurgated. His friend and former curate at Littlemore, W. J. Copeland, agreed to superintend the

1. *A.W.*, p. 258

publication in eight volumes, and spoke in the preface of how the sermons had 'acted like a leaven, on the mind and language and literature of the Church in this Country', and 'marked an era in her History'. He hoped and believed that they would do like good once more. To protect Newman from certain Catholics, it was explained also that since the sermons were printed entire and unaltered, 'they cannot be free from passages which he would now wish were otherwise, or would, one may be sure, desire to see altered or omitted'.[1] A little later, Copeland published a large selection from the eight volumes, with the explicit purpose of bringing Anglicans and Catholics together. 'I think we quite agree, Newman wrote to him on 13 October 1877, 'that the object of the selection is to cultivate a unity of ethos among those who otherwise differ', and in his preface Copeland expressed the hope that the volume would be welcomed, because those sermons had been included in it which 'from their bearing on the information of the Christian character may best contribute to the promotion of mutual sympathy between estranged communions and alienated hearts'.[2]

The republication of *Parochial and Plain Sermons* in 1868 was only the beginning. During the ensuing years Newman took in hand his other works. On 20 April 1873 he wrote to Copeland:

You have been of the greatest use to me in the matter of the sermons, and I only regret you have had so much trouble; but you have not had it for nothing. Unless you had broken the ice, I could have republished nothing which I wrote before 1845–6. The English public would not have borne any alterations—and my own people would have been much scandalized had I made none. They murmured a good deal at the new edition of the Sermons, as it was—but since you, not I published them nothing could be said about it. After this beginning, I took courage to publish my Essays on Miracles, and the British Critic Essays, uncorrected, but with notes corrective of the text. This too made some disturbance but very little—and then I published at Rivingtons my University Sermons—and then I went on to mix Anglican and Catholic Essays together—and now I hear no criticisms on these measures at all —and I have even dedicated a volume of my historical sketches, half of it written as an Anglican, to an Irish Bishop. My view has ever been to answer, not to suppress, what is erroneous—merely as a matter of expedience for the cause of truth, at least at this day. It seems to me a

1. *P.S.*, I, pp. vii–ix
2. *Selection adapted to the Seasons of the Ecclesiastical Year from the Parochial and Plain Sermons*, London 1878, p. vi

bad policy to suppress. Truth has a power of its own, which makes its way.[1]

In 1877 Newman republished *Lectures on the Prophetical Office of the Church viewed relatively to Romanism and Popular Protestantism.* This required a number of corrective notes, as has been seen, in which Newman answered his former self. He republished it as the first volume of *The Via Media of the Anglican Church*, with a new and important preface, eighty pages long. This he wrote for the sake of those who found much to admire in the Catholic Religion and believed its fundamental teachings, but whose consciences would not allow them to become Catholics. They felt unable to join the Church on account of the difference which at first sight presents itself between its formal teaching and its popular and political manifestations', as shown in its extravagant devotions or sentimental prayer books on the one hand, and in its narrow retrograde outlook in public affairs exemplified in 'the Sermons or Addresses of ecclesiastics in high position' on the other. Newman admitted that: 'It is so ordered on high that in our day Holy Church should present just that aspect to my countrymen which is most consonant with their ingrained prejudices against her, most unpromising for their conversion.' He explained that just as Christ is Priest, Prophet and King, so Christianity is a religion with its worship centred round pastor and flock, a theological teaching with its Schools, and a government with its Papacy and Curia. Devotion is the instrument of religion, and it tends to superstition, reasoning of theological enquiries, and it tends to rationalism, power of government, and it tends to ambition and tyranny. These three offices, the Sacerdotal, the Regal and the Prophetical, which ideally should balance each other, come into collision, and the interests of either truth or devotion or stable rule suffer in consequence. Newman shows by historical examples how theologians have been too hard and intellectual, the Papacy too neglectful of theology and too ready to be guided by expedience. Yet theology has a certain jurisdiction over the Regal and Sacerdotal offices, for it is commensurate with Revelation, and Revelation is the initial and essential idea of Christianity.[2]

By the end of 1877 Newman had republished in the uniform

1. Quoted by John Coulson in *Newman: a Portrait Restored, an Ecumenical Revaluation*, London 1965, pp. 112–16
2. *V.M.*, I, pp. xxxvii and xlvii

edition all his Anglican writings (apart from a few minor ones), with the exception of the *Treatises of St Athanasius*. These, which owing to interruptions were not completed until 1881, were somewhat altered in form, the text being in the first volume and the revised notes, some of them short essays, in the second. Thanks to this arrangement, it was easy to discover Newman's own view, the notes being in alphabetical order, under such headings as 'Catholic: the Name and the Claim', 'The Father Almighty', 'The Divine In-Dwelling', 'The Blessed Mary', 'Scripture', 'The Holy Trinity in Unity'. The republication of all his works in this uniform edition, Newman undertook, as has been seen, with a very definite end in view. Works which would perhaps have been reprinted only for scholars now had a second life, and acted as a levelling force among Catholics and Anglicans.

Besides these labours Newman had his tasks in the Oratory at Birmingham, which was being strengthened with new members, including two sons of his friend, Serjeant Bellasis. This meant increased work for the Superior, while the Oratory School remained an anxiety in the years following the death of Ambrose St John. Newman preached to the boys on Sundays, gave religious instruction to the senior boys, and at the end of each school year helped to coach the actors in the Latin play, Terence or Plautus, which he had edited. Besides this there was the constant stream of visitors to the Oratory, some seeking counsel, others, those friends who had gathered round him at every period of his life. Friends were lost or drifted away, but the phenomenon first remarked at Trinity, although it can be traced even earlier at Ealing School, of close friends collected round Newman and delighting in his company, continued right to the end of his life. It is perhaps worth remarking that these included a host of lay people, not only men, but whole families. In spite, or rather because of, what one of them described as his 'singular chivalrous courtesy mingled with an indescribable reserve' towards women, he was on terms of close friendship and corresponded confidentially with a dozen or more of them, about equally divided between married and single.

The immense correspondence showed no sign of slackening. Newman regarded it as one of his most important pastoral labours. After the *Apologia*, when he was once more a well-known figure, respected for his understanding and his integrity, men and women of all religions and none, turned to him for enlightenment and guidance. Some twenty thousand of the letters Newman wrote during his long life have been preserved. He became famous so early that they were kept from the time of the Oxford Movement, and, of course, they were kept also for their intrinsic interest and beauty. When all are printed, they will fill some thirty large volumes. They bring us in touch with Newman himself more closely than any of his works. It becomes possible to know him almost like a living friend, and in spite of his reserve, they reveal his natural, energetic, humorous and practical character. It was one of his sayings that there is a right way and a wrong way of doing everything, and in his letters we can see him trying, not necessarily with success, year in and year out, to do things the right way.

The end of 1877 found him still fully occupied, and with his visitors and correspondents to show how much *individuals* appreciated him. Suddenly, when his life seemed almost ended, there came *official* recognition. In December 1877, the President of his first College, Trinity, wrote to ask if he would become the first honorary Fellow. The College proposed to exercise for the first time its power of making such appointments. Newman replied at once:

No compliment could I feel more intimately, or desire more eagerly at once to seize and appropriate than that which is the subject of your letter just received. Trinity College is now, and ever has been, in my habitual thoughts. Views of its buildings are at my bedside and bring before me morning and evening my undergraduate days and those good friends, nearly all now gone, whom I loved so much during them and my love for whom has since their death kept me in affectionate loyalty to the College itself.[1]

It was sixty years to the day since he had gone up to Oxford with his father, and been entered at Trinity. He revisited the College in February 1878, his first visit to Oxford since he had left for good in 1846. He dedicated to the President and Fellows of Trinity the new edition of the *Development of Christian Doctrine*, first published as he left Oxford, and republished when he recovered a position there.

In the same month of February 1878 Pius IX died and Leo XIII was elected Pope. It seems that the idea of making Newman a Cardinal originated with him. A few years later at an audience given to Newman's friend, Roundell Palmer, first Lord Selborne,

1. Henry Tristram, *Newman and his Friends*, London 1933, p. 202

and his daughter, he called him 'Il mio Cardinale. It was not easy, they said he was too liberal; but I determined to honour the Church in honouring Newman'. At any rate, the idea was at once taken up by the Duke of Norfolk and some of the English laity, who approached Leo XIII. A year later in 1879, Newman was made a Cardinal, but only after what, now that all the correspondence has come to light, seems definitely to have been a last-minute manoeuvre of Manning's to prevent it. Newman said nothing, and indeed, just as he had kept as silent as possible over his differences with Faber, so he did, in the decades that followed, over those with Manning. So much was this the case, that, when Purcell's *Life of Cardinal Manning* was published in 1895, the story told there of the long opposition between the two men came as a revelation to members of Newman's own Oratorian Community. By a privilege unique in those days, Newman was to remain at his Oratory in Birmingham, and would be neither a Cardinal with a diocese nor a Cardinal in Curia. His elevation was a providential vindication of all he stood for. He could no longer be called 'half a Catholic', or 'unsound', or the preacher of 'a mutilated form of Catholicism'. In the speech he made at Rome, when receiving the official summons, he explained what the work of his life had been: 'For 30, 40, 50 years I have resisted to the best of my powers the spirit of liberalism in religion. Never did Holy Church need champions against it more sorely than now.' He then gave a definition: 'Liberalism in religion is the doctrine that there is no positive truth in religion. . . . It is inconsistent with any recognition of any religion as *true*. Revealed Religion is not a truth, but a sentiment and a taste. . . . Devotion is not necessarily founded on faith.' But this champion of Revealed Religion could appreciate the good in what he opposed, and he added: 'It must be borne in mind, that there is much in the liberalistic theory that is good and true; for example, not to say more, the precepts of justice, truthfulness, sobriety, self-command, benevolence. . . . It is not till we find that this array of principles is intended to supersede, to block out, religion, that we pronounce it to be evil.'[1]

Newman was seventy-eight when he was made a Cardinal, and the last eleven years of his life were spent in comparative peace, with his growing Community, his school, his many visitors, and his correspondence. He was still anxious to do what he could to

1. *Ward*, II, pp. 460 and 462

help on Revealed Religion. The great difficulty of the day was the reconciliation of the new scientific discoveries with the truth and reliability of Holy Scripture. This was a great critical and also a great pastoral problem. It was one that Newman had wrestled with in 1860–1, in papers that he did not feel able to publish in the atmosphere of those days. The problem was now more urgent than ever, and he wrote an article in *The Nineteenth Century* for February 1884, on 'Inspiration in its relation to Revelation'. He took the broad view that the freedom from error which covered Holy Scripture as a religious document did not necessarily cover scientific and historical *obiter dicta*, although it did include matters of faith and morals and the history bound up with them. It was long before his main insight was accepted, but the Second Vatican Council vindicated it, when it described the Bible as teaching 'without error that truth which God wanted put into the sacred writings for the sake of our salvation'. At the time, this honest effort to meet what was a great crux to so many people produced a not over-courteous answer from a professor of Scripture at Maynooth. He misrepresented Newman's thesis, and claimed that 'its startling character' must be evident to 'the merest tyro in the schools of Catholic Theology'. Newman, anxious to keep the question an open one, replied, holding to his position, and when the professor was made an Irish bishop shortly afterwards, sent him a present.[1]

Thus he went on working to the end. Francis Joseph Bacchus, who after being at the Oratory School, became one of Newman's Oratorians in 1881, wrote of him forty years after his death that he 'carried the art of being ordinary to perfection. He took his food, his recreation, went about his ordinary duties, conversed without any mannerisms whatsoever. He had no foibles, no crotchets'. Bacchus was surprised at his 'patience under annoyances of the kind which do try old people, such as noise, being kept waiting, forwardness on the part of young people'.[2] Lord Coleridge, the Chief Justice, whose testimony to Newman's influence during the Oxford Movement has been quoted earlier, wrote in 1882:

> I cannot analyze it or explain it, but to this hour he interests and awes me like no other man I ever saw. He is as simple and humble as a child,

1. *Stray Essays on Controversial Points*, pp. 1–65
2. *The Eighteen-Eighties*, edited by Walter de la Mare, Cambridge 1930, quotations on pp. 71–2

and, yet, I am with a being unlike anyone else. He lifts me up for the time, and subdues me—if I said frightens me it would hardly be too strong; and if he does this to a commonplace old lawyer, what must it be to men who can really enter into him and feel with him.[1]

As a Cardinal, Newman used to stay regularly with Dean Church, at the deanery of St Paul's. After the visit in 1886, Church wrote to Edward Talbot, then Warden of Keble: 'Well, I dare say you have heard that we had three days of the Cardinal. He was so bright, so kind, so affectionate . . . he was quite alive to all that is passing around him, though cautious and reticent as he should be. But the old smile and twinkle of the eye, and the bright meaning *eironeia*, are all still there. . . .'[2] Church, like Bacchus, remarked on Newman's naturalness, which 'has no doubt to do with good taste and good manners, but it has as much to do with good morals—with the resolute habit of veracity with oneself—with the obstinate preference for reality over show, however tempting—with the wholesome power of being able to think little about oneself'.[3]

Dean Church, too, remarked on how English Newman was,

. . . with all his quickness to detect and denounce what was selfish and poor in English ideas and action, and with all the strength of his deep antipathies, his chief interests were for things English—English literature, English social life, English politics, English religion. He liked to identify himself as much as possible, with things English, even with things that had belonged to his own first days. He republished his Oxford sermons and treatises. He prized his honorary fellowship at Trinity; he enjoyed his visit to Oxford, and the welcome which he met there. He discerned how much the English Church counted for in the fight going on in England for the faith in Christ. There was in all that he said and did a gentleness, a forbearance, a kindly friendliness, a warm recognition of the honour paid him by his countrymen, ever since the *Apologia* had broken down the prejudices which had prevented Englishmen from doing him justice.[4]

Newman died on 11 August 1890, and two days later Dean Church began the obituary in the *Guardian* with the following paragraph:

1. E. H. Coleridge, *Life and Correspondence of Lord Coleridge*, II, pp. 313–14
2. Mary Church, *The Life and Letters of Dean Church* London 1894, p. 321
3. R. W. Church, *Occasional Papers*, II, pp. 479–80
4. *Op. cit.*, p. 477

Cardinal Newman is dead, and we lose in him not only one of the very greatest masters of English style, not only a man of singular purity and beauty of character, not only an eminent example of personal sanctity, but the founder, we may almost say, of the Church of England as we see it. What the Church of England would have become without the Tractarian Movement we can faintly guess, and of the Tractarian Movement Newman was the living soul and the inspiring genius. Great as his services have been to the communion in which he died, they are as nothing by the side of those he rendered to the communion in which the most eventful years of his life were spent. All that was best in Tractarianism came from him—its reality, its depth, its low estimate of externals, its keen sense of the importance of religion to the individual soul. . . . He will be mourned by many in the Roman Church, but their sorrow will be less than ours, because they have not the same paramount reason to be grateful to him.[1]

Since those words were written, Newman's influence has spread wide and deep in the Catholic Church. This has become obvious since the new 'openness' began by Pope John XXIII, and continued in the Second Vatican Council, which has even been acclaimed as 'Newman's Council'. Like Pope John, he was fond of insisting, 'in necessariis unitas, in dubiis libertas, in omnibus caritas'. Certainly his protests against Catholic Novatianism, 'narrowing the lines of communion', and Catholic Nihilism, replying to urgent needs merely by prohibitions, no longer fall on deaf ears.[2] He wanted Catholics to come out of the ghetto and take their place in the world, to adapt themselves, to enlarge their minds in the confidence that truth could never contradict truth, and to be guided like responsible men by their duly enlightened consciences. His views on faith, on free discussion, on the Church as a Communion, on the place of the laity whether in the Church or the world, and many other points, are now appreciated, as are his return to the source of Revelation and his effort to make real the spiritual teaching of the New Testament. This last was meant not for sheltered groups but for those living in the world, a spirituality for the baptised. In apologetics his strength lies in his ability to see and state the objections. He has supreme confidence in the power of truth, yet his defence is humble, and does not pander to intellectualism at the expense of mystery. His life was a sacrifice for the

1. This passage is quoted in *The Correspondence of John Henry Newman with John Keble and Others*, pp. 389–90
2. *Ward*, II, pp. 127 and 486

truth. He was the apologist *par excellence* of the Church, who abandoned so much that he loved in the English Church, only to face misunderstanding and opposition in the Church of his adoption. All through he was buoyed up by his trust in Providence. Before he was sixteen he had come to the realisation that God was truly personal and always present. The Presence and Providence of God was perhaps the lesson on which this champion of Revealed Religion insisted most. Although the unseen world was so vivid to him, he yet knew the limitations of Revelation, and asked to have inscribed on his memorial tablet the words, 'Ex umbris et imaginibus in veritatem', 'Out of shadows and images into the truth'. Long before, he had pointed out in a lecture to the medical students of his University, how

> . . . physical nature lies before us, patent to the sight, ready to the touch, appealing to the senses in so unequivocal a way that the science on which it is founded is as real to us as the fact of our personal existence. But the phenomena, which are the basis of morals and Religion, have nothing of this luminous evidence. Instead of being obtruded on our notice, so that we cannot possibly overlook them, they are the dictates either of Conscience or of Faith. They are faint shadows and tracings, certain indeed, but delicate, fragile, and almost evanescent, which the mind recognizes at one time, not at another,—discerns when it is calm, loses when it is in agitation. The reflection of sky and mountains in the lake is a proof that sky and mountains are around it, but the twilight, or the mist, or the sudden storm hurries away the beautiful image, which leaves behind it no memorial of what it was. Something like this are the Moral Law and the informations of Faith, as they present themselves to individual minds.[1]

1. *Idea*, p. 514

Bibliography

THE great majority of Cardinal Newman's works he collected himself into the uniform edition, between 1868 and 1881. From 1886 until the stock was destroyed in World War II it was published by Longmans, Green and Co. This edition is being reproduced photographically by Christian Classics Inc. Westminster, Maryland. It includes:

(1) *Parochial and Plain Sermons*, eight volumes, first published 1834–43; *Sermons on Subjects of the Day* and *Sermons Preached before the University of Oxford,* both first published in 1843; *Discourses to Mixed Congregations*, 1849; *Sermons Preached on Various Occasions*, 1857.

(2) The main treatises: *The Arians of the Fourth Century*, 1833; *Lectures on the Doctrine of Justification*, 1838; *An Essay on the Development of Christian Doctrine*, 1845; *The Idea of a University*, 1852–9; *An Essay in aid of a Grammar of Assent*, 1870.

(3) Controversial: *The Via Media of the Anglican Church*, two volumes, of which the first is a republication of *The Prophetical Office of the Church*, 1837, with notes and an important Introduction, 1877, and the second a collection of Essays and Tracts, 1830–41; *Certain Difficulties felt by Anglicans in Catholic Teaching*; two volumes, the first reproducing the Lectures of 1850, the second including *A Letter to Pusey on Occasion of His Eirenicon*, 1866, and *A Letter to the Duke of Norfolk on Occasion of Mr Gladstone's Expostulation*, 1875; *Lectures on the Present Position of Catholics*, 1851; *Apologia pro Vita Sua*, 1864.

(4) Historical: *Historical Sketches*, three volumes, the first including *Lectures on the Turks* and part of the *Church of the Fathers*, the second the main part of the *Church of the Fathers*, also *St Chrysostom* and the *Mission of St Benedict*, the third *Rise and Progress of Universities* and *Northmen and Normans in England and Ireland*; *Select Treatises of St Athanasius*, 1842; *Tracts: Theological and Ecclesiastical*, chiefly patristic.

(5) Essays and novels: *Two Essays on Miracles*, 1826 and 1842; *Discussions and Arguments*, including *The Tamworth Reading Room*, and *Who's to Blame*, about the English race and the Crimean War; *Essays Critical and Historical*, two volumes; *Loss and Gain*, 1848; *Callista*, 1855; *Verses on Various Occasions*, 1867.

There are paperback editions of the *Apologia*, *Idea of a University*, *Development of Doctrine*, *A Grammar of Assent*, *Loss and Gain*, *Callista*. Also *A Letter to the Duke of Norfolk* was republished in 1964, and there are two or three recent volumes of selections from the Anglican Sermons, C. F. Harrold began a new edition of the Works in 1947, but it was cut short by his death.

Stray Essays on Controversial Subjects, privately printed 1890, includes the 1884 article on the Inspiration of Scripture. In 1961, John Coulson edited, with a penetrating introduction, the article *On Consulting the Faithful in Matters of Doctrine*, 1859.

Since Newman's death there have been published *Meditations and Devotions of Cardinal Newman*, 1893 (which includes *Meditations on Christian Doctrine*), often reprinted; *My Campaign in Ireland*, 1896; *Addresses to Cardinal Newman and his Replies*, 1905; *Sermon Notes of John Henry Cardinal Newman*, 1913; *Autobiographical Writings*, 1956; *Catholic Sermons of Cardinal Newman*, 1957.

It is hoped in the near future to publish a volume containing Newman's Philosophical Notebook, another containing his Oratorian Papers, Chapter Addresses and Papers on the Religious Life, and at least two further volumes of Theological Papers.

Newman's life is best studied in his own letters: *Letters and Correspondence of John Henry Newman during his Life in the English Church*, edited at Cardinal Newman's request by Anne Mozley, 1891; *Correspondence of John Henry Newman with John Keble and Others, 1839–45*, edited at the Birmingham Oratory, 1917; and for the Catholic period, Wilfrid Ward, *The Life of John Henry Cardinal Newman, based on his private journals and correspondence*, 1912. In 1961 there began to appear what it is hoped will be the complete edition of *The Letters and Diaries of John Henry Newman*. The series was inaugurated by Volume XI, October 1845–6, edited at the Birmingham Oratory by the present writer. Five further volumes have been published, two with the help of V. F. Blehl, S.J.: with Volume XVI October 1855 has been reached.

Maisie Ward has completed her father's standard biography, with *Young Mr Newman*, 1948. The fullest biography of Newman, based on the primary sources and eminently readable, is that of Meriol Trevor, *Newman, the Pillar of the Cloud*, and *Newman, Light in Winter*, both 1962. Notable short biographies are R. H. Hutton, *Cardinal Newman* 1891, and L. Bouyer, *Newman his Life and Spirituality*, 1958. More specialised are H. Tristram, *Newman and His Friends*, 1933; F. L. Cross, *John Henry Newman*, 1933; J. M. Flood, *Cardinal Newman and Oxford*, 1933; R. D. Middleton, *Newman and Bloxam*, 1947, and *Newman at Oxford*, 1950; Sean O'Faolain, *Newman's Way*, 1952; *Newman Family Letters*, edited by Dorothea Mozley, 1962; Jean Honoré, *Itinéraire spirituel de Newman*, 1964.

The best general introduction to Newman's thought is the article in *Dictionnaire de Théologie Catholique*, 1931, by Joseph Bacchus and Henry Tristram. Also Charles Frederick Harrold, *John Henry Newman*, 1945, A. J. Boekraad, *The Personal Conquest of Truth*, 1955, and *The Argument from Conscience to the Existence of God*, 1961, J. H. Walgrave, O.P., *Newman the Theologian*, 1960; James Collins, *Philosophical Readings in Cardinal Newman*, 1961; J. M. Cameron, *The Night Battle*, 1962; J. H. Harper, *Cardinal Newman and William Froude*, 1933 (correspondence); Owen Chadwick, *From Bossuet to Newman*, 1957 (on Development); Jean Guitton, *La Philosophie de Newman*, 1933; M. Nédoncelle, *La Philosophie Religieuse de Newman*, 1946; H. Fries, *Die Religionsphilosophie Newmans*, 1948; A. Läpple, *Der Einzelne in der Kirche, Wesenzüge einer Theologie des Einzelnen nach John Henry Newman, 1952*; Luca Obertello, *Conoscenza e Persona nel Pensiero di John Henry Newman*, 1964

For Newman and education see A. Dwight Culler, *The Imperial Intellect, a Study of Newman's Educational Ideal*, 1955; Fergal McGrath, S.J., *Newman's University, Idea and Reality*, 1951, and *The Consecration of Learning*, 1962; *Theology and the University*, edited by John Coulson, 1964, 'Newman's Idea of an Educated Laity—the Two Versions'; F. Tardivel, *J. H. Newman Educateur*, 1937, and *La Personalité Littéraire de Newman*, 1937; Wolfgang Renz, O.S.B., *Newman's Idee einer Universität*, 1958.

On special subjects: H. Laski, *Studies in the Problem of Sovereignty*, 1917; Terence Kenny, *The Political Thought of John Henry Newman*, 1957; Günter Biemer, *John Henry Newman on Tradition*, 1966; N. Schiffers, *Die Einheit der Kirche nach Newman*, 1956; F. J. Friedel, *The Mariology of Cardinal Newman*, 1928; F. M. William, *Aristotelische Erkenntneslehre bei Whately und Newman*, 1960; Edward Bellasis, *Coram Cardinali*, 1916; W. R. Lamm, *The Spiritual Legacy of Newman*, 1934; G. Velocci, C.S.S.R., *Newman Mistico*, 1964.

There are interpretations of Newman in R. W. Church, *Occasional Papers*, II, 1897; H. Bremond, *The Mystery of Newman*, 1907; Wilfrid Ward, *Ten Personal Studies*, 1908, and *Last Lectures*, 1918; D. G, James, *The Romantic Comedy*, 1948; John Holloway, *The Victorian Sage*, 1953; J. Coulson and A. M. Allchin, *Newman: A Portrait Restored: an Ecumenical Revaluation*, 1965. Among anthologies are *A Newman Synthesis*, arranged by Eric Pryzwara, S.J., 1930, reprinted as *The Heart of Newman*, 1964, *A Newman Treasury*, chosen by C. F. Harrold, 1945; *Newman, Prose and Poetry*, selected by Geoffrey Tillotson, 1957; *The Essential Newman*, edited by Vincent Ferrer Blehl, S.J., 1963; *A Newman Companion to the Gospels*, by A. J. Coupet, O. P., 1966.

R. W. Church, *The Oxford Movement*, 1891, is still the best account.

Among innumerable other books concerning it are Y. Brilioth, *The Anglican Revival*, 1925; Christopher Dawson, *The Spirit of the Oxford Movement*, 1933; J. A. Froude, 'The Oxford Counter-Reformation,' in *Short Studies on Great Subjects*; G. Faber, *Oxford Apostles*, 1933; *The Mind of the Oxford Movement*, edited by Owen Chadwick, 1960; Horton Davies, *Worship and Theology in England*, IV, *From Newman to Martineau*, 1962; S. L. Ollard, *A Short History of the Oxford Movement*, 3rd edition 1963. Also C. C. J. Webb, *Religious Thought of the Oxford Movement*, 1928; Alf Härdelin, *The Tractarian Understanding of the Eucharist*, 1965.

Other books that illuminate Newman's history are R. Aubert, *Le Pontificat de Pie IX, 1952*, new edition 1963; Owen Chadwick, *The Victorian Church*, 1966; the biographies of contemporaries, especially C. Butler, *The Life and Times of Bishop Ullathorne*, 1926, and E. S. Purcell, *The Life of Cardinal Manning*, 1896; also P. Thureau-Dangin, *The English Catholic Revival in the Nineteenth Century*, 1915; E. E. Y. Reynolds, *Three Cardinals*, 1958; Josef Altholz, *The Liberal Catholic Movement in England*, 1962; Hugh A. MacDougall, O.M.I., *The Acton-Newman Relations*, 1962; *Ignaz von Döllinger Briefwechsel mit Lord Acton I 1850-1869*, edited by Victor Conzemius.

Useful articles on Newman, in various languages, and bibliographies, are published in *Newman Studien*, of which the first volume appeared in 1948, and the sixth in 1964. Works on Newman are reviewed at length in the annual *Philosophical Studies*, edited at Maynooth.

Index

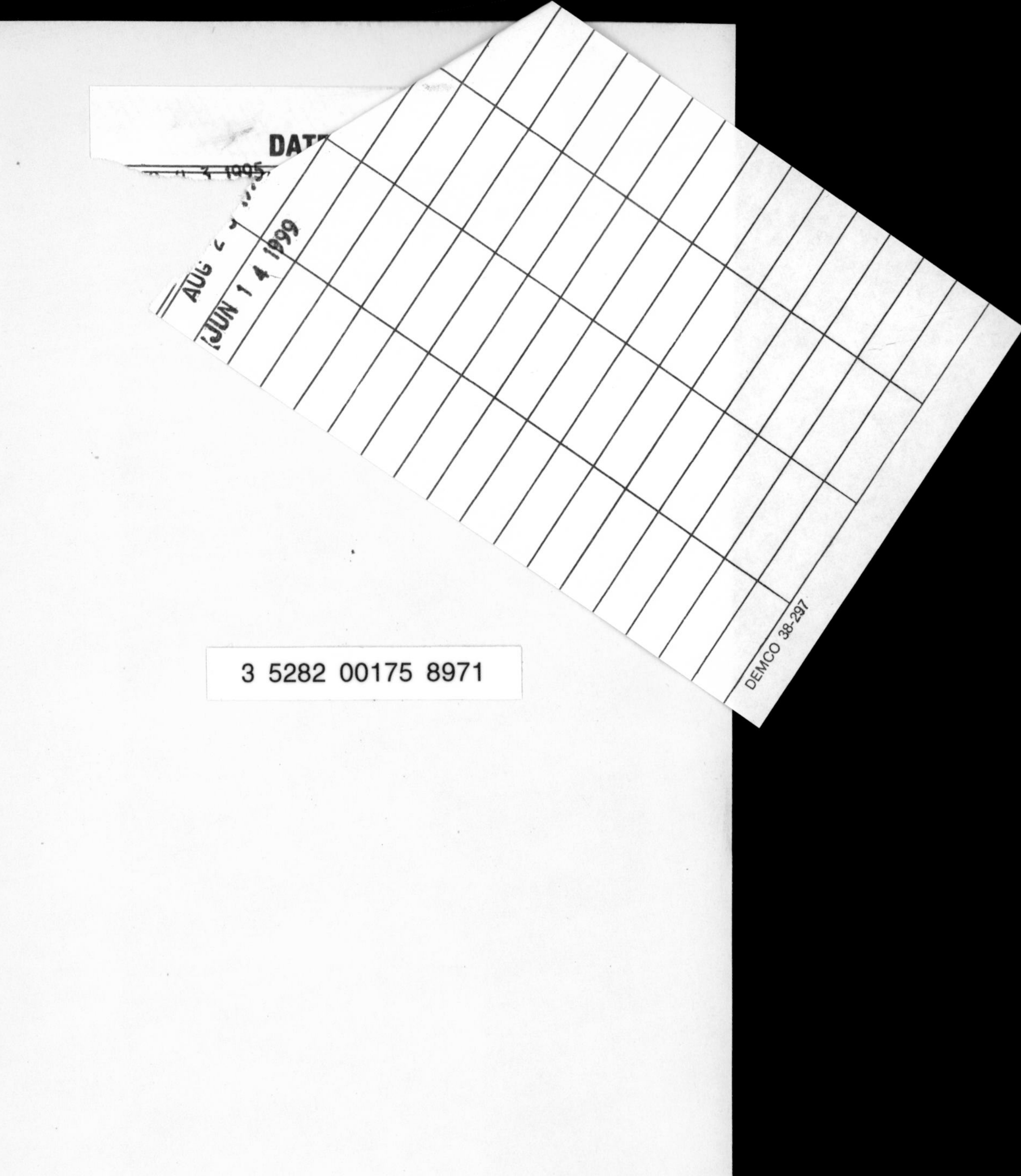
DAT
JUN 1 4 1999
DEMCO 38-297
3 5282 00175 8971